TABLE FOR TWO

Books by Shirley Sarvis

COOKING SCANDINAVIAN
(with Barbara Scott O'Neil)

SAN FRANCISCO FIREHOUSE FAVORITES
(co-author)

A TASTE OF PORTUGAL

CRAB & ABALONE

TABLE FOR TWO

TABLE FOR TWO

Shirley Sarvis

ILLUSTRATED BY BARBARA O'NEIL ROSS

Garden City, New York

DOUBLEDAY & COMPANY, INC.

1968

To my parents

Library of Congress Catalog Card Number 68–18094
Copyright © 1968 by Shirley Jean Sarvis
All Rights Reserved
Printed in the United States of America
First Edition

1455760

Contents

Recipes for items followed by † can be located by
consulting the Index.

Introduction

Cooking for two is the happiest kind of cooking. It lets you concentrate on the food and not the serving; it assures good company; it is an opportunity for the unorthodox; it insists that the menu be of few but fascinating items; it invites a flourish and encourages innovation; it is not bound up in rules. And it is wonderfully romantic just by nature.

It encourages utter devotion to the care of your one chosen guest—and smooths the way to all the affection and romancing that such gentle attention implies. It's terribly cozy and comfortable for two lovers (or nearly so) to plot together their most special eating delights, then delight in them together. And when you happily satisfy the palates of two people already willing to get along well, you add a marvelous dimension to the promise of the situation; because the world glows rosier all about.

Two dining out has been such a successful courtship ruse for so long; but it only portends the romantic potential of two dining in.

Cooking is the one art form that is utterly social. And the socializing of just two can often bring that art form to its best form. The social situation of two eating is a perfect time for eating for romance and recreation and not nutrition. It lets you take an excursion into glorious tasting rather than simply into food.

Cooking for two demands simplicity. And that simplicity lets you put things together in non-clichéed ways.

It gives you a chance to cook to reveal your tastes—

and yourself. Cooks like to cook the way they like to eat. With only one other taste to please, this is your chance.

This book sets a table for two in many ways. These tables for two are mainly for cook and courter. But they are also for the generous gesture when a guy cooks for his gal, a wine breakfast to welcome an overnight guest to a new day, a long-talk lunch with a best friend suddenly in love, a candle-light dinner for a married pair, or even a sensational supper for Uncle Alfred in town on business, or soup and sherry with Aunt Agnes just home from a trip.

This book is not just a recipe book; it is a plotting book—with menus. It is a guide for cooking for two, not just a collection of recipes for two.

But beyond this, it can also be an inexperienced cook's training ground. A success in cooking for two builds confidence for future cooking for more. The book is written with some recipes throughout that you can simply and safely multiply to expand for four or six or eight guests. These are the recipes for a beginning cook to learn on two and, later, put into use on more guests. (Expandable recipes and any special directions for expanding them are indicated by an asterisk *.)

A major approach of the book is that, next to intriguing food, atmosphere makes a successful eating occasion—and confidence is the cook's key to radiating an easy ambiance. One way to achieve confidence is to be original. Do things *your* way; break new ground—and you and your cooking can't be candidates for comparison. So you can cook with freedom and *your* confidence. Another simultaneous way to keep confident is to do what you can handle comfortably. Keep within the scope of your culinary talents, financial means, and serving setting (but don't try to keep within your experience, or cooking will be boring).

Another attitude of this book: few items to eat make for the most drama—and the most appreciation of those items from your audience. This is even intensified in cooking for two: simple efficiency in terms of quantities of materials you use and results you get makes it much more satisfying to cook with a quantity of ingredients that will bring one flamboyant result, rather than working with tiny proportions of ingredients to make many little dishes, none of which can possibly be large enough to make a memorable impression. The point is to cook one or two wonderful things, not a lot of less than exciting things.

The method is to concentrate on one or only a few items and dramatize them. The focal item could be your culinary specialty; you can show it off by serving it nearly alone (for example, if crab bisque is your best soup, have it your *pièce de résistance* and surround it with just good bread and wine). The major item could be one favorite dish that you long for and consider a treat and feel the urgency to share (plan a twosome occasion around beef tartare—if that is your current passion, or Brandy Alexanders—if that is your momentary whim among beverages). It could be a splendid food of the season (dill-boiled crayfish, cold beer, and dark bread; or the rich fruitcake Aunt Mildred always sends at Christmas time —with a good Port du Salut and a chilled light muscat wine; or a grape pie baked in the short Concord season—served warm and à la mode).

All this is linked to your own cook's confidence. Having few items on a menu lets you lean upon your culinary specialty (or specialties). And a few things instead of many call for relatively slight preparations—to make small demands upon you. Let the idea reign, not the work.

Practically every one of the recipes in this book is simple; if it is not, it is possible to do ahead of time except for last-minute finishing, so that any complicated cooking is long out of the way by the time your guest arrives. Still, this book is not for those who do not like to cook—and to eat. This book is for you who want to do good cooking, not some form of get-by or acceptable cooking. (You will not find among these recipes TV-dinner and mushroom-soup-sauce short cuts. In most cases, from-scratch cooking is just as fast as "convenience" ways, much more joyful to do, far more creative and rewarding, and supremely superior to eat.)

Do start with good ingredients. A compromise in quality of ingredients is no compromise; it is an absolute submission to mediocrity and an out-and-out invitation to dissatisfaction.

Menus in this book are simple and unconventional. The drama is in the striking combination (beef, bourbon, and bitters, for example) and the goodness of the dishes (a fine old-fashioned, a crusted-outside, rare-inside broiled steak sauced with a bitters-butter whip).

This book is divided by *ways* or *ideas* of eating, not by items and occasions.

In using it, don't be bound by any chapter barricades. Let ideas lap over: a Gougère and wine Significant Snack could easily be a Two Cooks project or a Midnight Breakfast. Or the Carrot Curry Soup among Soup and Pie Suppers could be just Soup and Something to Sip—with sherry. The roast Cornish game hens with ham interlining and cream cheese sauce do not have to be Little Roasts; they could be a Midnight Breakfast idea but changed to some late supper. . . .

You will find some cross-referencing of recipes from one chapter to another; good dishes have more than one fine use.

Every recipe has been tested in minimal space and with the minimal utensils (as outlined in Chapter 1, Starting Out).

Unless otherwise noted, all recipes are written to yield two servings.

And each recipe and menu idea has been tried and tasted with at least one twosome guest—with a happy outcome.

Starting Out

This is the specific-advice chapter for getting started. It is the planning before the party; the thought before the thrill; the little effort before the entertainment and eating; the anticipation before the action.

It gives you a short list of essential equipment you'll need for cooking, serving, and eating—in terms of two. It comments on cooking and serving in small spaces, gives a cooking-term glossary, and considers before-dinner eating and drinking.

EQUIPMENT

Getting outfitted for cooking for and serving two is no big undertaking. Just buy a few well-thought-out, good-quality, multiuse items.

Try to get things that will work for cooking *and* serving *and* eating. For example, get small custard cups that you can use for baking muffins and popovers and custards and puddings and eggs, and also use for serving these custards and puddings—and desserts, vegetables, sauces, and condiments.

Be warned that when you look over the housewares section of almost any department store, you will find multitudes of little pots and pans and baking dishes and serving platters that are charming and reasonably effective to use when cooking for two. But these are nonessential and additions that you can make on your own; they are not listed here.

The following list is of basic, necessary equipment. As many pieces of it as possible are in standard sizes, so that these pieces can, if necessary, and/or at another time, be useful for cooking for more than two.

I usually choose a large piece of equipment over a small one—as in the case of frying pan, double boiler, saucepan, casserole—on the theory that you can always cook a small amount in a big pot; it's pretty difficult to do the reverse.

Heavy deep casserole with cover, about 3½ to 4 quarts, that can cook on top of the stove or in the oven, and can come to the table. It might be of enamel-coated iron or steel, cast iron, Teflon, Pyroceram. Perhaps this is the single most important piece of equipment of all. It is certainly your most important pot (and likely to be most expensive). But it is all-purpose. It is your Dutch oven, baking casserole, stewpot, and fish kettle all in one. In a pinch, it can be a frying pan or a mixing bowl. And it is the serving vessel for all you've cooked in it and more. So don't skimp on quality or style. It should be something you'll be happy living with.

Heavy frying pan with cover, about 9-inch diameter. Possibly (and hopefully) the frying pan and your deep all-purpose pot (above) can be of the same set, so that one lid will top them both.

Double boiler, about 2 to 2½ quarts. Use bottom part and lid to fill your need for a saucepan with cover.

2 individual big bowls or soup plates or casseroles or deep skillets or large individual ramekins—or anything wide and shallow and heatable in the oven and, if possible, on top of the stove. These are for generous individual servings of stew, a big soup, or a nested chop or piece of meat or fish, or a salad bowl. They may also be the cooking utensils for the above items; they can even be bread-baking pans for individual loaves. Capacity of each should be about 3 cups.

Crêpe pan, 7- or 8-inch diameter. More commentary in The Party
Crêpe chapter.

Roasting pan, about 15 by 10 inches, with rack. Use rack also
as cooling rack.

Wooden board, 12- by 12-inch minimum, with two work surfaces. Keep one side exclusively for the savory things: chopping onions, herbs, slicing fish, etc.; keep the other side for
subtly and sweetly flavored activities: rolling out pastries
and doughs, kneading bread dough, slicing oranges, etc.

Cutlery. Three good knives can see you through. But be sure
they are excellent quality stainless steel or carbon steel.
Quality is more important in cutlery than at any other point
of equipment buying; a cheap knife is never a bargain.

> French knife with 9-inch blade. One big French knife is
> enough because one large one can do all the cutting, chop-
> ping, and mincing that it *and* a retinue of succeedingly
> smaller knives can do.

> Carving knife with 8- to 10-inch blade.

> Thin-bladed paring knife.

Wire strainer, about 1-quart size. Use as strainer and sifter.

Small electric mixer.

Wire whisk. (Nice to have; not essential: be sure it is flexible.)

Rotary beater.

Electric blender. You can survive without it. But you can live
the good life with it.

Large slotted spoon.

Kitchen fork.

Kitchen shears. Just have them at hand and you'll find how much
you need them.

Can opener. For this generally noncan cooking, the dime-store,
twist-by-hand type is fine.

Vegetable peeler.

4-sided metal grater.

Garlic press.

3 ovenware glass measuring cups, 1-quart, 1-pint, and 1-cup sizes. These double as beating and mixing bowls.

Set of 4 metal level-measuring cups, 1-cup, ½-cup, ⅓-cup, and ¼-cup sizes.

Set of 4 measuring spoons, 1-tablespoon, 1-teaspoon, ½-teaspoon, and ¼-teaspoon sizes.

Set of 3 ovenproof mixing bowls, about 2½-quart, 1½-quart, and 1½-pint sizes.

Six 5-ounce custard cups.

1 baking sheet, about 15 by 12 inches.

1 loaf bread pan, about 9 by 5 inches.

7-inch spring-form pan.

8-inch square baking pan.

8-inch pie pan.

Rolling pin.

Pastry blender. If you're a stickler for the uncluttered life, you *can* skip this, and use two knives instead. But life is far smoother with it.

1 rubber spatula (scraper). Two are better than one.

1 flexible baking spatula, about 8-inch blade.

1 pancake turner.

Circle biscuit cutter, about 2-inch diameter.

Large wooden spoon for stirring doughs and batters. Do not use this for stews (and soups and sautés), or the onion-and-garlic and pungent-savory seasonings of your stew may later sadly season your delicate, sweet mixtures.

2 large trays, about 14-inch diameter or 16 by 12 inches. Use as serving trays and, more often perhaps, as eating trays—each tray as one person's table, place mat, and plate-liner all in one.

Coffee maker. I prefer 8-cup heatproof glass filter type.

Carafe or pitcher. For ice water, jug wine, beer, milk.

Large salad bowl with servers.

Salt shaker.

Pepper grinder.

Ovenproof serving platter, about 12 by 9 inches or equivalent.

Large serving fork.

Large serving spoon.

Sauce ladle.

Cream and sugar servers.

2 tulip-shaped wineglasses, at least 8-ounce size.

2 large, heavy sundae glasses, about 1¼-cup size. These should
be heavy, so they seem significant to hold, and so you can
chill them and they'll hold their chill. Thumb-printed Hoff-
man House-style beer goblets are ideal and inexpensive.
These are for sundaes, chilled soups, seafood cocktails, heady
beverages, and small desserts that seem especially special
when they are dwarfed in big glasses.

2 large dinner plates that can be heated in the oven.

2 salad plates.

2 bread-and-butter plates.

2 dessert plates.

2 coffee cups and saucers.

2 soup or dessertspoons.

2 dinner forks.

2 dinner knives.

4 salad and/or dessert forks.

4 teaspoons.

2 long-handled iced tea or sundae spoons.

COOKING AND SERVING IN SMALL SPACES

It is pretty much accepted and expected that cooking for two and cooking and serving in small spaces happen simultaneously.

I do not see cramped quarters and little equipment as necessarily a plight or a deterrent to good cooking. In fact, I think these circumstances are assets, particularly when you're cooking for two: they force efficiency; they force simplicity. They save a cook cooking steps and dishwashing.

These suggestions may help ease a cramped kitchen:

Hide the dessert in the bedroom until ready to serve.

Use those cubic inches of oven space for storage space. *Caution:* the oven is great for storage (particularly for dishes that you've prepared just up to the point of baking before your guest appears)—only if you condition yourself to check what is in there *every* time before you turn it on.

In moments of squeezed despair, keep reminding yourself of the major advantage of small space: you can stay in one place and reach and do almost everything.

When you are serving in a small apartment or any eating area of wee footage, you may find these suggestions helpful:

Use trays—one tray for each person—and let each tray serve as a whole table setting—table, place mat, dinner-plate-liner; and carry your table setting around wherever you need it for eating.

Make a coffee table a dining table, and sit on cushions.

Keep the décor on small tables small. A little mug of bright flowers and a single candle are enough. Or three fruits arranged in a leaf-lined basket. Or a tiny piece of sculpture set on a cluster of fresh green leaves. Or simply a bright-colored fabric table runner.

GLOSSARY OF COOKING VERBS

For beginning cooks, here is a brief glossary of basic cooking terms as they are used in this book and in most other cookbooks.

bake – to cook by dry heat in oven. Always preheat oven.

baste – to moisten food while it is cooking (as meat while roasting) by spooning liquid or fat over it.

beat – to mix with a vigorous motion with spoon, whip, or beater. Purpose is to blend or make smooth or incorporate air.

blend – to mix thoroughly.

boil – to cook in steaming liquid in which bubbles are breaking on surface.

broil – to cook directly under heating unit or over fire.

cream – to soften by beating with mixer or by rubbing mixture against a bowl with a spoon until mixture (usually shortening and sugar) is light and fluffy or creamy.

cut in – combine shortening and flour or dry ingredients with pastry blender or two knives.

fold – to combine gently by bringing rubber scraper down through mixture, across bottom, up and over top until blended.

fry – to cook in hot fat.

knead – to work dough with a motion of pressing and pushing dough away with heels of hands to stretch it, folding dough forward, and repeating pressing and pushing away to stretch.

marinate – to let food stand in a seasoning liquid.

pan-broil – to cook uncovered in ungreased or lightly greased hot frying pan, pouring off grease as it accumulates.

poach – to cook in simmering (not boiling) water or other liquid.

purée – to press fruit or vegetables through a fine sieve or whirl in a blender. Or the resulting thick mixture.

roast – to cook by dry heat.

roll out – place on board and spread thin with a rolling pin.

sauté – to brown or cook in a small amount of fat in frying pan.

scald – to heat to temperature just below boiling point.

score – to cut narrow gashes part way through outer surface of food.

sift – to put through a fine sieve or flour sifter.

simmer – to cook in liquid just below boiling point on top of stove.

steam – to cook in the steam that rises from boiling water or other liquid.

toast – to brown by direct heat.

toss – to mix ingredients lightly without crushing them.

whip – to beat rapidly to produce expansion by incorporating air, as in egg whites and whipping cream.

MEASURING NOTES

Flour. One cup sifted flour means 1 cup sifted regular all-purpose flour measured level. (For quick measuring, you can skip sifting: lightly spoon flour up several times in its storing container to loosen, then spoon lightly into measuring cup.)

Eggs. Recipes have been tested with eggs that are size-graded as large.

Equivalents: 3 teaspoons in 1 tablespoon
16 tablespoons in 1 cup
8 fluid ounces in 1 cup

DINNER INTRODUCTIONS—
TO DRINK AND TO EAT

This is territory for personal likes and tastes to take over. I often find it simplest and most conducive to food appreciation to let hors d'oeuvres be only a few nuts or olives or a cutting of good cheese; and let the drinks before dinner be the dinner wine or dinner beer. However, there are also plenty of times when the perfect bigger drink (or so) before dinner is the only way to lead up to the food comfortably and satisfyingly. You know your guests and those times. But even with a major cocktail, I still hold out for unpronounced hors d'oeuvres and just enough to offset alcohol and hunger and to *appetize*—so your dinner food will get maximum enjoyment.

Here are some of my favorite quick and not too filling appetizers:

Salted roasted macadamia nuts or almonds.

Finger sticks of mellow natural cheese lightly dusted with *fines herbes* or another favorite blend of dry herbs.

Cherry tomatoes.

Cherry tomatoes cut almost in two, each filled with a smoked oyster (canned, well drained) and toothpicked shut. Garnish serving plate with parsley.

Garlic olives from a Greek or Italian delicatessen.

Thin, crisp Italian breadsticks with a pot of butter beaten to a whip and seasoned with chopped fresh parsley or other herbs you choose. Use butter as a dip for breadsticks. Have more breadsticks with plain butter with the main part of the meal.

Raw mushrooms, rinsed, dried, and thickly sliced. Stack in a small bowl, and serve as you would nuts.

A small brick of cream cheese (on a board with a knife) with chopped fresh parsley or other herbs or dry herb blend pressed over all the surfaces. Spread on sesame or rye crackers.

Washed red radishes (halved if large) with a leafy handle left on, heaped in a bowl and served with sweet or salted butter to pile onto each.

Large chilled shrimp (cooked, shelled, deveined) with a dipping sauce made of catsup mixed with a dash of Pernod.

Fresh fennel stalks cut into 3- to 4-inch lengths and spiced with a light spreading of blue or Roquefort or other blue-veined cheese.

Little Roasts

For purposes of this book, "roasts" means practically anything you bake in the oven—from a one-rib prime rib roast to sole fillets.

But roast also means a relatively major piece of meat. Don't let that valuable item frighten you. Intimidating though a solid chunk of meat may be to an inexperienced cook, it is really about the best place to begin cooking. Because it is really the easiest cooking of all: just put it into the oven.

While you're roasting a roast, you can also be cocktailing with your suitor, and attending to his predinner comforts (not the demands of some complicated dinner delicacy)—irrefutable arguments for learning roasting first.

Two matters of main importance in the roast realm:
(1) The piece of meat you start with
(2) Timing

For the first, my most important advice to any cook is this: cultivate a good meat man. A friend in a butcher shop is worth at least six other kinds of friends if you value good eating. His understanding of your special interest in fine food and his good sense and advice are priceless.

For the second, be particularly attentive to recipe direction. Whenever roasts are large enough, use a meat thermometer. And as you keep cooking, develop your natural and common-sense sense of timing. One rule I like is, "When you start to smell it, it's nearly done." Granted, that sounds like the most useless guide. But once you start applying it, you find it has an almost uncanny accuracy. It works when you're simmering a soup, sautéing vegetables, baking a cake. But it is probably most useful with roasting since, with a large roasting item, timing takes more gravity than with something smaller. And the more tests you have for doneness, the more safe things seem. Certainly the sniffing test is not sufficient alone. But it is a good supportive one.

SHERRY GLAZED SPARERIBS AND ARTICHOKES

All you need with this is a smooth red table wine and corn bread or French bread.

SHERRY GLAZED SPARERIBS AND ARTICHOKES

1 side pork spareribs (about 2 pounds), cracked to separate end ribs	3 tablespoons minced or grated fresh onion (or 2 tablespoons instant minced onion)
Salt and freshly ground black pepper	1 clove garlic, minced or mashed
1 can (8 ounces) tomato sauce	½ teaspoon Worcestershire sauce
½ cup each dry sherry and honey	1 package (about 9 ounces) frozen artichoke hearts, thawed just to separate
2 tablespoons wine vinegar	

Sprinkle spareribs generously on both sides with salt and pepper. Place in shallow roasting pan, and bake in a hot oven (400°) for 40 minutes. Drain off accumulated fat. Mix together remaining ingredients except artichokes, and pour over spareribs. Reduce oven temperature to 350°, and bake ribs for 40 minutes more, basting occasionally. Add artichokes to roasting pan, and stir into sauce to coat. Bake for 10 minutes more or until artichokes are tender. Arrange spareribs on serving platter with artichokes and sauce spooned over.

CORNISH GAME HENS WITH HAM INTERLINING

Roast one Cornish game hen per person. Perch the brace of them on a bed of watercress, and surround with small roasted potatoes. Serve chilled sliced oranges for salad and a light-bodied but smooth red wine.

Italian *prosciutto* interlines the flesh of each bird. Peppered cream cheese makes the stuffing and saucing; as you eat, fork it over meat and potatoes.

CORNISH GAME HENS WITH HAM INTERLINING

2 *rock Cornish game hens, about 1 pound each*	*Freshly ground black pepper*
Salt	*About 2 tablespoons melted butter*
4 *ounces very thinly sliced Italian prosciutto or ham*	6 *small new potatoes, peeled*
4 *ounces (half of large package) cream cheese, softened*	

Thaw game hens if necessary. Sprinkle cavity of each lightly with salt. Loosen skin from flesh over breast and back of each bird by gently slipping fingers between, reaching from neck and body openings. Insert *prosciutto* slices so they cover breast and back meat of each bird. Mix cream cheese and about ¼ teaspoon coarsely ground pepper, and spoon half into body cavity of each bird. Close body and neck openings with small skewers. Place birds, breasts up and slightly separated, with wing tips tucked behind shoulders, on rimmed baking sheet. Brush with melted butter. Coat potatoes with melted butter, season with salt and pepper, and place alongside birds. Bake in a moderate oven (350°) for 50 minutes or until bird leg joints move easily. Baste occasionally with melted butter. Remove skewers.

DEVILED SHORT RIBS

Short ribs seem about the beefiest of the beef cuts. With these, I have liked cooked leaf spinach for a vegetable, crisp cucumber sticks for a relish-salad, and tangy dried apricots in a compote or tart for dessert. Red wine.

DEVILED SHORT RIBS*

3 pounds beef short ribs, cut into serving pieces
Salt and freshly ground black pepper
1 small onion, coarsely chopped
About 3 tablespoons water

About 1 tablespoon each vinegar and melted butter
Fine dry bread crumbs
Chopped fresh parsley
Bottled devil sauce (Sauce Diable) (or vinegar or fresh lemon juice)

Place ribs in heavy frying pan or shallow casserole. Bake in a hot oven (425°) for about 30 minutes, until browned on both sides; turn once. Pour off accumulated fat. Season meat generously with salt and pepper. Add onion and water to baking pan. Cover and bake in a moderate oven (350°) for 1½ hours or until meat is tender. Discard onion and juices in pan. Sprinkle meat surfaces with vinegar, brush with melted butter, and coat with crumbs. Continue baking, uncovered, until crumbs are crisp and brown, about 30 minutes. Sprinkle with parsley. Serve with devil sauce (or sprinkle with vinegar or lemon juice).

PARMESAN GOLDEN SOLE

The soup-salad *gazpacho* makes a freshly cold accompaniment for hot, oven-roasted, Parmesan-crusted fillets of sole. Together, they make a supper.

PARMESAN GOLDEN SOLE

   6 tablespoons soft butter
   ¾ cup grated or shredded Parmesan cheese
   2 large fillets of sole, about ½ pound each

Spread half the butter thickly over bottom of baking-serving platter; sprinkle with half the Parmesan. Arrange sole in a single layer over cheese; dot with remaining butter; sprinkle with remaining Parmesan. Bake in a hot oven (400°) for 15 minutes or until cheese is golden; baste frequently with melted butter and cheese. Serve with drippings spooned over.

QUICK GAZPACHO

1 cup tomato juice
¾ teaspoon salt
¼ teaspoon each sugar and crumbled dried orégano
2 tablespoons each olive oil and white wine vinegar
1 clove garlic, minced or mashed

2 green onions with part of green tops, thinly sliced
1 cucumber, peeled, seeded, and finely diced
½ green bell pepper, finely diced
Garlic croutons

Combine all ingredients except croutons. Cover and chill for 4 hours. At serving time, ladle into soup or salad bowls, and sprinkle with a few croutons.

GLAZED HAM LOAF ROAST

This is a good deal more elegant than a common ham loaf, though it can't escape the common label. It is gentle and rich and subtle.

Serve hot, carved thick slices bordered with spiced peaches and with a whipped cream-horseradish sauce to spoon over and melt in. Fill out the menu with hot buttered rolls and a dry rosé. For salad later, toss torn lettuce leaves, thinly sliced peeled cucumbers, and a lot of lightly toasted, finely chopped walnuts with an oil-and-vinegar dressing seasoned with scraped fresh onion and mustard.

Chill the ham loaf that is left over, and serve it sliced for sandwiches or with potato salad.

GLAZED HAM LOAF ROAST*

1 pound uncooked smoked
   ham, ground
¾ pound fresh pork,
   ground
½ cup cracker meal or
   crushed saltine cracker
   crumbs

1 egg, beaten
½ cup hot milk
½ cup syrup drained from
   spiced peaches

Thoroughly mix together the ground ham and pork and crumbs. Mix in egg, then milk. Pat evenly into 9- by 5-inch loaf pan. Pour on as much syrup as the loaf will absorb. Bake in a moderate oven (350°) for 1½ hours, basting occasionally with remaining peach syrup. Cool in pan for about 10 minutes before carving.

HORSERADISH WHIPPED CREAM

Beat ¼ cup heavy (whipping) cream until stiff. Fold in about 1½ teaspoons prepared horseradish, ½ teaspoon sugar, and ¼ teaspoon fresh lemon juice. Turn into serving bowl. Chill for 2 hours before serving. Makes about ½ cup, enough for 2 servings.

* Bake double recipe in 11- by 8-inch pan.

HUNGARIAN VEAL SHANK BAKED IN SOUR CREAM

Add caraway to the meal seasoning one way or another: add about 1 teaspoon whole caraway seeds to sour cream sauce for veal. Or serve caraway noodles: cook egg noodles, drain, and toss with melted butter and caraway to season.

Make a salad vegetable: cook about ½ pound fresh green beans, French-cut (cut lengthwise into thin strips), covered, in boiling salted water just until tender, about 10 minutes (or cook 1 package [9 ounces] frozen French-cut green beans just until tender); drain. Shake or beat together ⅓ cup salad oil, about 2 tablespoons white wine vinegar, ½ teaspoon each sugar and salt, and about ⅛ teaspoon coarsely ground black pepper. Pour over hot beans, and let stand for 1 hour.

Wine: a full-bodied and -flavored white.

HUNGARIAN VEAL SHANK BAKED IN SOUR CREAM

1 veal shank (2 to 2½ pounds), cut in half crosswise

Salt and freshly ground black pepper

1 medium-sized onion, finely chopped

2 tablespoons butter

¼ pound fresh mushrooms, thinly sliced

1 large clove garlic, minced or mashed

1 tablespoon paprika

½ teaspoon salt

1½ cups commercial sour cream

4 tablespoons chopped fresh parsley

Season veal generously with salt and pepper. Place in greased roasting pan or casserole. Cover (with foil or casserole lid), and bake in a moderate oven (350°) for 1½ hours or until tender. Meantime, sauté onion in butter until limp. Add mushrooms; cover and simmer for about 5 minutes, stirring occasionally. Stir in garlic, paprika, and salt. Remove from heat, and stir in sour cream and 2 tablespoons of the parsley; pour over veal. Bake, uncovered, for 15 minutes more; spoon sauce over meat once or twice. Sprinkle with remaining parsley.

GARLIC LAMB CHOP ROASTS

Roast two double-thick loin lamb chops rare, as if each were a miniature loin roast. At the same time, bake savory accompanying Parmesan eggplant. Marinate both beforehand. Fill out a dinner menu with green salad, bread, and red wine.

GARLIC LAMB CHOP ROASTS

2 *double-thick loin lamb chops (each about 2 inches thick)*	*Olive oil*
	Salt and freshly ground black pepper
1 *clove garlic, split*	

Rub lamb surfaces with garlic, and brush with olive oil. Let stand for 30 minutes. Place, standing on bone end, fat side up, in shallow pan. Bake in a hot oven (400°) for 20 minutes (longer for medium or well done). Season generously with salt and pepper.

BAKED PARMESAN EGGPLANT

1 small unpeeled eggplant
(about 1 pound), cut
into ½-inch-thick
crosswise slices
3 tablespoons olive oil
1½ tablespoons wine
vinegar

½ teaspoon salt
¼ teaspoon crumbled dried
orégano
About 3 tablespoons catsup
About ½ cup grated or
shredded Parmesan cheese

Arrange eggplant slices in a single layer in a shallow baking pan. Shake or beat together oil, vinegar, salt, and orégano to make a dressing, and spoon half of it over eggplant surfaces; let stand for 15 minutes. Turn eggplant over, and spoon remaining dressing over; let stand 15 minutes. Spread top sides of eggplant slices with catsup; sprinkle with cheese. Bake in a hot oven (400°) for 20 minutes.

STANDING RIB ROAST FOR TWO

It *is* possible to have a standing rib roast for just two. You freeze it first, then roast it to the doneness you prefer. A food-consultant friend, Beatrice Ojakangas, worked out the fine points and facility for this special-occasion roast—even the bookend-like potatoes that bake along with the beef.

Add a leafy salad, red wine, butter for your potatoes (and possibly bread), and a green vegetable if you wish.

The timings here are approximate. The only way to measure doneness accurately is with a meat thermometer.

STANDING ONE-RIB BEEF ROAST FOR TWO

> 1 *rib of standing rib roast,*   2 *large baking potatoes,*
>   *about 2½ pounds*   *well scrubbed*
> 1 *tablespoon olive oil*
> 1 *small clove garlic, minced*
>   *or mashed* (*optional*)

Wrap meat well in freezer foil; freeze until solid. Remove
foil. Combine olive oil and garlic and rub over frozen meat.
Stand meat on bone end (fat side up) in a shallow roasting
pan, propped into position by a potato at each side. (If necessary, crumple a little foil to help hold meat in standing
position.) Bake in a hot oven (400°) for about 1 hour, 15
minutes for rare; 1 hour, 25 minutes for medium; and 1 hour,
35 minutes for well done. (After 1 hour's roasting, insert meat
thermometer through fat to center of roast, and continue
roasting until meat is done to your preference.) Let stand
for 5 minutes. Carve roast in two from top down to bone.
Cut along bone to free each piece.

One Dramatic Potful

This chapter is about the stew or casserole that is a whole dinner in a kettle—or almost so.

Each potful idea is calculated to let you think of cooking just that one potful for dinner and not much else—except your fondness for your invited friend.

A culinary theory behind the scheme is that, in a big pot, you have more of everything mingling with more of everything else—so that every flavor in the mélange (and in the meal, since it is all in one pot) is brought to even fuller taste by its large-area association with every other flavor. There is a certain difficulty of proving that theory that I find most intriguing. Perhaps it is pondering or tasting for that notion fulfilled that makes me so enthusiastic about the one potful idea.

But that enthusiasm is also because one potful is easy—and easily dramatic. You fill the pot full of chosen items; cook them together; add the striking finish, garnish, or accompaniments; and ladle the drama out of the pot. You can do the cooking well before serving time and the finishing at the last.

At your table for two, place the promise-filled pot on a handsome tray or trivet; and give it drama, dominance, and dressing with a swirl of brightly colored napkins or fabric around it, or a border of heavy leaves and some dry pods or pine cones, or an encirclement of low and fat or tall and thin candles. Keep any side dishes off to the side so that the pot keeps its position of prestige. Have the softening embellishment be goblets of wine and the glow of candles—and the ardor of two lovers for each other and what's in the pot.

The one potful idea is a dramatization of one of the main pleasures of cooking for two (and not for more): you don't have to repeat the motions of cooking so much that they become boring. You do each preparation activity so you get to sense it, and just enough so it is pleasurable and interesting and satisfying. You do not have to stand, browning meat for a stew forever to get the quantity you need; one layerful browned in the bottom of your casserole does it. You chop one onion, not one after another. You mince a little parsley, not a whole chopping board full. . . .

The one potful is where your core piece of equipment, that great heavy casserole, comes into full glory.

Remember that practically every stew or casserole is better for being made ahead by a day or a few hours, then reheated before serving. You can apply that principle to advantage to these that follow, except for the Mushroom Rice Milanese (and to that if necessary).

SPINACH LAMB CURRY WITH FRESH FRUIT CONDIMENTS

The cut fresh fruits serve as salad, curry condiments, and dessert.

Serve the spinach lamb over coconut rice made by cooking long-grain white rice with butter and grated coconut to season.

For bread, you might spread sturdy French-style bread slices with a ground cardamom-butter mixture, and heat it.

Pour a not quite dry but forceful rosé wine.

SPINACH LAMB CURRY WITH FRESH FRUIT CONDIMENTS

1¼ pounds boneless lean lamb, cut into 1½-inch cubes

3 tablespoons butter

1 large onion, very thinly sliced

2 teaspoons mustard seeds

1½ teaspoons each ground coriander and ginger

1 teaspoon ground turmeric

½ teaspoon chili powder

About ½ teaspoon salt

⅛ teaspoon crumbled dried thyme

1 package (10 ounces) frozen chopped spinach

About ½ cup plain yogurt

¼ cup water

Fresh fruit condiments (recipe below)

In a heavy casserole, brown lamb in 1 tablespoon of the butter over medium heat; remove from casserole; discard drippings in casserole. Add remaining butter to casserole; add onion, and sauté until limp. Return meat to casserole along with mustard seeds, coriander, ginger, turmeric, chili powder, salt, and thyme; sauté over medium heat for 5 minutes. Add spinach, 2 tablespoons of the yogurt, and water. Cover and simmer for about 1½ hours or until meat is very tender, stirring occasionally. Taste and add salt if necessary. Top each serving with a big spoonful of yogurt. Pass fresh fruit condiments.

Fresh fruit condiments • Cut fresh fruits of your choice into large pieces and arrange on a tray. Sprinkle all fruits lightly with chopped fresh (or crumbled dried) mint and each fruit with an appropriate spice (suggestions follow). Chill. Garnish with mint sprigs, cucumber slices, and lime wedges (squeeze lime juice over meat and fruits as you eat). Spice pineapple fingers with ground ginger, fig halves with mace, plum halves or quarters with coriander, orange slices with cinnamon, peach wedges with cardamom.

MOROCCAN CHICKEN AND ALMOND TAJIN

Set an exotic Moroccan scene for this little dinner for two. Call upon an Arabian Nights theme for mystery and romance. You, as hostess, wear a graceful long grown or a sweeping caftan. And play the subservient, please-the-master, harem-like role.

At dinner, you and your sultan-type dinner guest sit on fat pillows on the floor or at low-couch level—at a small, low table. Light by candle.

Before dinner, you soothe and refresh your gentleman guest: place before him a pretty basin and pour lukewarm water out of an elegant pitcher—over his hands and fingers (upcoming eating utensils); and offer a lace-edged linen towel for drying.

Then arrange the *tajin* on one large serving platter on the little table, flanked by one platter of salad and a basket of coarse-textured white (or near white) bread (spiced with a few whole fennel seeds, if you bake it yourself). And arrange the two of you together on those sumptuous cushions. You eat with your fingers, pulling off pieces of the melting-tender *poulet*, dipping them into the velvety sauce beneath. It's a courtesy for the lady to pluck off the choicest pieces and present them to her guest—and he can reverse the courtesy to keep this sharing-of-the-loveliest-things a two-way affair. (One hand is the rule for plucking and dipping and eating—for the initiated. But for two mutually helpful beginners, it is also a rule of courtesy for one to hold the chicken steadily while the other strips off the meat.) Each of you break off a small piece of the bread, and use it to scoop the condiment-like salad up onto it for eating.

No wine—if you want to be Moslem-authentic all the way. But I recommend a lot of very cold and fairly full dry rosé.

After the *tajin*, have fresh fruits of the season and, if you wish, some purchased Middle Eastern-type honey pastries.

Small cups of dark roast coffee—or better—the Moroccan ending, mint tea: put 1 tablespoon green tea into a heated teapot. Add a handful of rinsed fresh mint leaves and stems and about ⅓ cup sugar. Pour in 2 cups boiling water. Cover and allow to steep for 8 minutes. Stir with a spoon, taste, and add sugar if necessary. Pour tea in a long stream from as high as possible (so the warm mint aroma fills the air) to fill glasses halfway full.

After all the eating is over, lave your sultan's hands again with fresh water, and gently caress them dry with a finger-tip towel. Then sprinkle him with orange blossom water (orange flower water in clear, fresh water) from your finger-tips and out of a crystal bowl floating a blossom.

Light sandalwood incense, and put on low-key background music—a little minor, and of lutes and tambourines.

MOROCCAN CHICKEN AND ALMOND TAJIN

¼ cup blanched whole
almonds

½ tablespoon butter

¼ cup olive oil

2 tablespoons butter

1 large onion, very thinly
sliced

½ teaspoon salt

About ¼ teaspoon coarsely
ground black pepper

About ⅛ teaspoon powdered
saffron

About ¹⁄₁₆ teaspoon
cayenne

1 chicken breast, split

2 frying chicken thighs (or
1 drumstick-and-thigh
joint, separated)

¼ cup muscat (or other)
raisins

1 teaspoon fresh lemon
juice

In a frying pan, sauté almonds in the ½ tablespoon butter until brown; set aside. Heat olive oil and the 2 tablespoons butter in a heavy casserole. Stir in onion, salt, pepper, saffron, and cayenne. Add chicken pieces, and turn to coat with onion mixture. Cover and simmer for 1½ hours or until chicken is very tender; turn chicken occasionally. Remove chicken to shallow serving platter; keep warm. Cook sauce in pan over high heat, stirring, until almost all liquid evaporates and until reduced to a thick sauce. Stir in raisins, lemon juice, and almonds, and heat through. Turn over chicken.

GREEN CHILE RELISH SALAD

1 can (4 ounces) green
chiles, cut into thin
lengthwise strips
1 large ripe tomato, peeled,
seeded, and finely
chopped
3 tablespoons finely
chopped parsley

1½ tablespoons olive oil
1 teaspoon fresh lemon
juice
About ½ teaspoon ground
cumin
About ¼ teaspoon salt

Stir together all ingredients. Taste and correct seasoning
with cumin and salt. Spread in a shallow layer on a salad
plate.

MUSHROOM RICE MILANESE

For a North Italian menu, the saffron *risotto* would probably be minor and a veal meat dish major. But if you make
the *risotto* lavish with dried mushrooms, it deserves all the
attention. The rice should be rather creamy and not dry.

Accompany it with chilled fingers of fresh melon and fresh
fig halves, spiral-wrapped with thinly sliced *prosciutto* (Italian
ham) and a slightly fruity white table wine. When fresh
melons and figs are not in season, serve with a chilled compote of poached plums or tart and sweet cherries.

If you must make rice ahead and reheat before serving,
cover it, and heat through in a moderate (350°) oven.

MUSHROOM RICE MILANESE

1 ounce (or more) dried mushrooms

1 large onion, finely chopped

5 tablespoons butter

¾ cup uncooked long-grain white rice

¼ cup white table wine

2 tablespoons Marsala (or medium sherry)

1 can (about 14 ounces) chicken broth (or 1¾ cups chicken broth) heated to boiling

Pinch of saffron powder

Grated Parmesan cheese

Soak mushrooms in hot water to cover until soft, about 30 minutes; squeeze dry, saving ¼ cup of the liquid; thinly slice. In a heavy casserole, sauté onion in 4 tablespoons of the butter until limp. Add rice and cook over medium heat, stirring, for about 3 minutes. Stir in mushrooms, reserved mushroom liquid, white wine, Marsala, and chicken broth. Cover and cook over low heat for 20 minutes or until rice is tender. Gently stir in remaining butter and enough saffron to season and to color rice a rich yellow. Sprinkle lightly with Parmesan.

CHILEAN CHICKEN AVOCADO

This potful is not hot. It is chicken chilled in aspic. You must do the cooking the night before the dinner.

As it simmers, the chicken takes up as much of the olive oil as it needs to become utterly smooth and almost nutty tasting. After the dish is cooked and cooled, you pour off the excess olive oil and combine it with vinegar and salt and pepper to make a dressing for an accompanying salad of broken romaine.

Add wine (chilled, not quite dry white) and bread (delicate hot corn muffins, perhaps) to round out the menu. For dessert, have hot chocolate stirred with a cinnamon stick.

CHILEAN CHICKEN AVOCADO

¼ cup olive oil

1 chicken breast, split

2 frying chicken thighs (or 1 drumstick-and-thigh joint, separated)

1 medium-sized sweet onion, cut into ⅛-inch-thick slices

2 large carrots, peeled and thinly sliced crosswise

1 can or jar (2 ounces) pimentos, drained and coarsely chopped

Salt

About 8 whole black peppercorns

1 can (13 ounces) clear consommé madrilène

¼ cup medium-dry white table wine

Lettuce leaves

1 small avocado, cut into lengthwise slices

Herb-orange mayonnaise (recipe below)

Pour olive oil over bottom of heavy casserole. Arrange chicken pieces in it, in a single layer, skin side down. Separate onion slices into rings and arrange one half of them over chicken; sprinkle with half the carrots and half the pimentos; sprinkle with salt to season and half the peppercorns. Top with remaining onion, carrots, pimentos, salt to season, and peppercorns. Heat madrilène to melt; mix with wine; pour over casserole contents. Cover casserole, and simmer for 1½ hours or until chicken is very tender. Remove from heat and allow to cool at room temperature. Then chill overnight. Next morning, pour off excess olive oil, being careful not to disturb casserole layering. Return to refrigerator for at least 1 hour. At serving time, unmold chicken in madrilène onto a chilled serving platter. (To unmold, loosen madrilène from casserole edges with a thin-bladed knife; dip bottom of casserole into warm water for a few moments—until you can gently shake contents loose. Place serving platter upside-down on top of casserole; invert casserole.) Tuck lettuce leaves around edges of jellied chicken. Arrange avocado slices in a border. Pass herb-orange mayonnaise.

Herb-orange mayonnaise • Stir together until smooth 6 tablespoons mayonnaise; 3 tablespoons commercial sour cream; 1 teaspoon grated fresh orange peel; ¾ teaspoon each dry mustard and lemon juice; ⅜ teaspoon crumbled dried thyme; and ³⁄₁₆ teaspoon crumbled dried orégano. Chill for 30 minutes or more.

The Greeks seem to have a mastery of the one potful idea. Here are two of them:

GREEK STIFADO

The beauty of this is that you don't have to brown the meat.

The salad: young fresh spinach leaves and coarsely chopped walnuts tossed and dressed with oil, lemon juice, salt, and pepper.

The cheese to eat with the stew and salad: Greek feta or another rather salty cheese such as medium-aged Monterey Jack or Parmesan or Gouda.

The bread: a sturdy white.

The wine: a robust red.

GREEK STIFADO*

1 to 1¼ pounds lean beef stew meat, cut into 1½-inch cubes	1 tablespoon dried currants (or 2 tablespoons raisins)
Salt and freshly ground black pepper	¼ cup dry red table wine
3 tablespoons butter	½ can (6-ounce size) tomato paste
½ pound small boiling onions, peeled	1 tablespoon wine vinegar
½ bay leaf	2 teaspoons brown sugar
1 small cinnamon stick	1 small clove garlic, minced or mashed (optional)
¼ teaspoon whole cloves	¼ teaspoon ground cumin

Season meat generously with salt and pepper. Melt butter in heavy casserole. Add meat and turn to coat on all sides with butter. Arrange onions, bay leaf, cinnamon, cloves, and currants (or raisins) over meat. Mix remaining ingredients and pour over casserole contents. Cover onions with a plate (to hold them intact). Cover casserole, and cook over very low heat for 3 hours or until meat is very tender. Do not stir. As you serve, stir sauce gently to blend.

LAMB AND ARTICHOKES AVGOLEMENO

They say in Greece that *Avgolemeno* is the cornerstone of the Greek kitchen. And you believe it when you see how that egg and tart-lemon sauce is almost ever present in the Greek cuisine, but in such diverse ways. Here it is the topping, thickening, and finishing sauce for a savory stew of lamb and artichokes.

* To increase recipe to 6 servings, double all ingredients above except use 3 pounds meat and 2 pounds onions.

You can make this stew ahead of time up to the point of adding vegetables and *Avgolemeno*.

Serve with this heavily sesame-buttered and toasted French-style bread and dry rosé wine. Later, you might drizzle some honey on more of that sesame-toasted bread for a suggestion of dessert.

LAMB AND ARTICHOKES AVGOLEMENO

1½ pounds boneless lean lamb, cut into 1½-inch cubes
2 tablespoons olive oil
Salt and freshly ground black pepper
1 medium-sized onion, thinly sliced
1 clove garlic, minced or mashed

About ⅜ teaspoon dried dill weed
½ cup water
1 package (8 ounces) frozen artichoke hearts, thawed just to separate
3 egg yolks
3 tablespoons fresh lemon juice
Chopped fresh parsley

In a heavy casserole, brown lamb over medium heat in 1 tablespoon of the olive oil; remove from casserole, and season generously with salt and pepper. Add remaining oil to casserole, add onion, and sauté until limp. Return meat to casserole along with garlic, dill, and water. Cover and simmer for 50 minutes or until meat is tender. Add artichokes to casserole, season with salt, cover, and simmer for 10 minutes more or until tender. Meantime, beat egg yolks until light and fluffy, and slowly beat in lemon juice and about 3 tablespoons of the hot liquid from lamb. Remove casserole from heat; gradually stir egg sauce into casserole juices. Cover and let stand for 5 minutes or until juices thicken slightly. Sprinkle with parsley.

1455760

PORTUGUESE LEMON PORK IN A POT

With this: a bright and light-bodied red wine to drink, cooked leaf spinach on the side, and sugared fresh orange slices for dessert.

Squeeze the fresh lemon juice generously over pork and potatoes.

PORTUGUESE LEMON PORK IN A POT

4 *pork rib chops, about*	2 *tablespoons olive oil*
1¼ *inches thick, boned*	4 *peeled small new potatoes*
and trimmed	*Salt and freshly ground*
4 *cloves garlic, minced or*	*black pepper*
mashed	2 *lemons, halved*

Rub meat surfaces with 2 of the garlic cloves. In heavy casserole, sauté remaining garlic in olive oil until golden. Add chops to casserole, and brown well on both sides over medium heat; push to side of pan. Add potatoes to casserole, and brown on all sides. Season meat and potatoes generously with salt and pepper. Cover and cook over low heat for 30 minutes or until meat is very tender. Stir pan drippings to loosen and blend, and serve over pork and potatoes. Garnish with lemons.

SZEGED GOULASH

This is one stew where the presentation can be almost more dramatic out of the pot—and in individual casseroles— than in it. Either way, you garnish each serving with a notched hard-cooked egg half and parsley; pass additional parsley-sprinkled sour cream to drop on top and stir in to taste.

Have a full red dinner wine. Make a salad of thinly sliced cucumbers salted and chilled to wilt, then drained and seasoned and dressed with bits of green bell pepper, salt, black pepper, sugar, and vinegar, and served garnished with tomato wedges. Add sturdy bread if you wish. Dessert could be chilled plums in a compote or a purchased tart or *torte* of plums or dried apricots.

SZEGED GOULASH

1 pound lean beef stew
  meat, cut into 1½-inch
  cubes
1 tablespoon butter
1 large onion, finely
  chopped
2 teaspoons paprika
1 small clove garlic, minced
  or mashed
¼ teaspoon each whole
  caraway seeds and
  crumbled dried marjoram
Grinding of black pepper
½ bay leaf

2 small smoked pork chops
  (or about ⅓ pound
  smoked lean ham, cut
  into large cubes)
¼ cup each dry red wine
  and water
2 small potatoes, peeled
  and cut into sixths
About ½ cup commercial
  sour cream
1 hard-cooked egg, cut in
  half crosswise in notched
  pattern
Chopped fresh parsley

In large casserole, slowly brown beef on all sides in butter. Add onion, and cook until limp. Stir in paprika, garlic, caraway seeds, marjoram, and pepper. Add bay leaf, smoked pork, wine, and water. Cover and simmer for 2½ hours or until beef is tender; stir occasionally. Add potatoes, and cook for 30 minutes more or until tender. Taste and correct seasoning with salt and pepper. Just before serving, stir 2 tablespoons sour cream into meat sauce. Garnish with hard-cooked egg and parsley. Pass remaining sour cream.

Soup or Stew and Something to Sip

In these combinations, menu simplicity is the main thing. The point is to catch the character of the soup or stew—and not be fettered by other taste sensations that are simply distractions. Another point is very little work for the cook.

The most enhancing thing for these soups or stews is not much—just the drink that counters and contrasts and a completing item or two. Eating and drinking this way make a case for the perfection of simplicity.

The nature of each soup or stew tells the time for it: a hot Danish fruit soup makes a warming dessert-supper. It makes an excuse for two of you to curl up around a warm fire late one cold winter's night—perhaps after a chilling-through walk in the icy outdoor air—then to delve into hot chocolate and a hot fruit-tart soup that floats and melts a great puff of whipped cream.

An avocado chili makes an autumn al fresco lunch. The time could be a sunny warm autumn midday, with the wind barely lifting the colored leaves to foretell the upcoming season, and you and your favorite friend comfily settled in that delicious outdoors, savoring hot avocado chili and drinking cold beer.

A rich crab bisque with sherry makes a Sunday supper on one of those quiet Sunday nights when the two of you want to be alone at your home, halcyon and happy together. You might settle on the floor with a single supper tray for you both, and slowly sip sherry and sup on crab soup, and let the world go on without you. . . .

CREAM-BROILED MUSHROOM SOUP
Dry White Wine

Choose a dry white wine with a gentle force and medium body, perhaps one of the Riesling types. Offer crisp buttered toast fingers.

CREAM-BROILED MUSHROOM SOUP

4 tablespoons butter
½ pound fresh mushrooms, thinly sliced
1 tablespoon fresh lemon juice
¾ cup chopped fresh parsley
1 can (about 10 ounces) beef bouillon

1 cup commercial sour cream
3 tablespoons dry white wine
Pinch of salt
¼ cup heavy cream, whipped

Melt butter in frying pan, add mushrooms, sprinkle with lemon juice, and sauté until lightly browned and tender. Stir in parsley. Add bouillon. Gradually add ¾ cup of the sour cream and the wine; heat slowly, stirring. Turn into two heatproof serving dishes. Fold remaining sour cream and salt into whipped cream; spoon on top of soup; broil (about 5 inches from heat) just until glazed with brown. Serve immediately.

OYSTER PAN ROAST
Cold Beer

This is modeled after the famed pan roast of the Oyster Bar in Grand Central Terminal. Nothing but beer will do to drink.

OYSTER PAN ROAST

1 jar (10 or 12 ounces) Eastern or small Pacific oysters, drained
6 tablespoons soft butter
2 tablespoons chili sauce
2 teaspoons Worcestershire sauce
½ teaspoon fresh lemon juice
About ¼ teaspoon celery salt

Freshly ground black pepper
Paprika
¾ cup heavy (whipping) cream
2 slices bread, toasted until dry in a slow oven and well buttered

Combine oysters, 2 tablespoons of the butter, the chili sauce, Worcestershire sauce, lemon juice, celery salt, a generous grinding of black pepper, and ⅛ teaspoon paprika in frying pan. Bring to a boil, and cook for about 1 minute or until oyster edges curl, stirring constantly and gently. Add cream, and return to boiling. Place toast slices in 2 wide soup plates, and ladle oysters and liquid over. Top with remaining butter, and sprinkle generously with more paprika.

AVOCADO CHILI CON CARNE
CORN BREAD
Crisp Apples   Monterey Jack, Teleme, or Münster
Beer

Chili and beer are the menu essentials. Corn bread is an embellishment to go with the chili and beer during the first part of the meal and to mingle with the apples and cheese at the last.

The cheese can be any young, creamy, slightly salty natural cheese.

As is true with most stews, this is a little better if you make it a few hours ahead, let it cool and settle and the flavors mellow, then reheat before serving.

AVOCADO CHILI CON CARNE*

1 pound ground chuck

1 medium-sized onion, finely chopped

About 2 teaspoons chili powder

About 1 teaspoon each salt, sugar, and dry mustard

About ½ teaspoon freshly ground black pepper

1 can (1 pound) stewed tomatoes

1 small can (about 8 ounces) small red kidney beans, drained

1½ teaspoons finely grated unsweetened baking chocolate

Thin lengthwise peeled avocado slices

In a casserole or frying pan, slowly brown ground beef in its own fat. When meat is brown, add onion, and sauté until limp. Add chili, salt, sugar, mustard, and pepper, and stir until well blended. Add tomatoes and beans. Cover and simmer for 20 minutes; stir occasionally. Add chocolate; stir until melted. Taste and correct seasoning. Turn into two shallow serving bowls. Arrange avocado slices over top.

QUICK CORN BREAD*

1 egg	½ cup sifted flour
½ cup milk	1 tablespoon sugar
3 tablespoons melted butter	2 teaspoons baking powder
½ cup yellow cornmeal	⅜ teaspoon salt

Beat egg in a mixing bowl. Stir in milk, butter, and cornmeal. Sift flour, sugar, baking powder, and salt into bowl. Stir just to moisten all ingredients. Turn into a buttered 9- by 5-inch loaf pan. Bake in a hot oven (400°) for 20 to 25 minutes or until edges are brown and top is golden.

* Bake double recipe in 9-inch square baking pan.

HOT FRUITS SOUP DANISH
Hot Chocolate
Whipped Cream

This soup is much like a Danish fruit soup, but easier. This menu is good for a late, small supper on a cold night, with freshly baked, crisp popovers an agreeable addition. For such an eating, pass a bowl of unsweetened whipped cream, and drop puffs of it onto fruits and hot chocolate.

If you do not serve popovers, add a few lightly toasted chopped almonds to the soup toppings.

HOT FRUITS SOUP DANISH*

⅔ cup dried apricots, cooked and drained
⅔ cup prunes, cooked and drained
1 cup orange juice
¼ cup firmly packed brown sugar
Pinch of salt
About 1 cup heavy cream, whipped
Ground cinnamon

Combine apricots, prunes, orange juice, brown sugar, and salt in a saucepan and heat through. Ladle into serving dishes. Top with whipped cream and a sprinkling of cinnamon.

Sip a sherry with your guest while the makings for the crab bisque marinate. Thereafter, you can make your little supper in a matter of maybe five minutes. And you won't need to tear yourself away from that irresistible guest for very long.

CRAB CURRY BISQUE
BUTTER BROWNED ENGLISH MUFFINS
Dry Sherry

CRAB CURRY BISQUE*

⅓ cup dry sherry
¼ pound (about ½ cup)
  flaked crab meat
1 can (about 10 ounces)
  green pea soup
1 cup half-and-half (half
  milk and half cream)

Curry powder to taste
  (about 1 teaspoon)
About ½ teaspoon
  crumbled dried basil
Chopped fresh parsley

Pour sherry over crab and let stand for 30 minutes. In a saucepan, blend together undiluted pea soup, half-and-half, curry, and basil. Heat slowly, stirring; do not boil. Add crab and sherry and heat through. Serve immediately, sprinkled lightly with parsley.

BUTTER BROWNED ENGLISH MUFFINS

Spread split English muffins generously with butter and broil-toast until butter browns.

ROYAL HAM AND NUTMEG BROTH
Hot Raisin Muffins or Buttered Toast
Chilled Rosé or White Table Wine

This is good for those evenings—perhaps after a large or late lunch—when you want something for dinner, but not much.

Select the wine for its full, fruity bouquet—perhaps a varietal rosé; or a California Chenin Blanc, Pinot Blanc, or white Pinot; or a Pouilly Fuissé, Pouilly Fumé, or Maconnais.

ROYAL HAM AND NUTMEG BROTH

1 can (about 14 ounces) chicken broth or 1¾ cups chicken broth
¼ cup very finely diced smoked ham
2 tablespoons uncooked rice
2 green onions with part of green tops, thinly sliced
2 egg yolks
2 teaspoons lemon juice
Ground nutmeg

Combine broth, ham, and rice in a saucepan; bring to a boil, cover, and gently boil until rice is tender, about 20 minutes. Add onions and heat through. Beat egg yolks well, then beat in lemon juice; gradually beat in about 3 tablespoons of the hot broth. Remove soup from heat. Beating constantly with a whisk, slowly add egg sauce to soup. Cover and let stand for 5 minutes, then serve immediately. Sprinkle very lightly with nutmeg.

GREEK FETA SHRIMP
Anise Bread
A Vigorous White Table Wine

To prepare anise bread, brush thick slices of whole-wheat or coarse white bread with melted butter and crushed anise or fennel seeds, and broil toast.

If you want salad, make it of lettuce and black olives tossed with oil and lemon juice.

Make and present this stew in a frying pan. The tomato in the center is mainly for show and optional. If necessary, you can substitute for the feta another meltable, rather salty cheese such as medium-aged Monterey Jack or Parmesan or Wisconsin Münster; add salt to taste.

GREEK FETA SHRIMP

1 *large onion, thinly sliced*	*About ¼ teaspoon freshly*
3 *tablespoons olive oil*	*ground black pepper*
3 *medium-sized ripe*	*⅛ teaspoon sugar*
tomatoes	*½ pound large raw shrimp*
2 *tablespoons chopped*	*or prawns, shelled and*
fresh parsley	*deveined*
About ¼ teaspoon dried	4 *to 6 ounces feta cheese,*
dill weed	*crumbled*
	Dill or parsley sprigs

In frying pan, sauté onion in olive oil until limp. Coarsely chop 2 of the tomatoes and add to frying pan along with parsley, dill weed, pepper, and sugar. Cover and simmer for 30 minutes, stirring occasionally. Dip shrimp into tomato sauce to coat, and arrange in a border around outside edge of pan; sprinkle with feta. Place whole tomato, core side down, in center. Bake in a very hot oven (450°) for 10 minutes or until shrimp loses translucency and cheese is melted. Tuck dill or parsley sprigs around base of tomato.

Skillet Suppers

There are those who hold that the only way to cook wisely for two is to broil everything.

I disagree—not only because I am put off by broiler-washing, but because I think that you can just as easily braise or simmer a whole meal in a kettle or sauté or pan-broil a whole meal in a skillet as you can broil in a broiler—and probably with more latitude of ingredients and less precision of cooking timing. For two, a frying pan is a better size than a broiler; it is easier to watch and handle (and wash).

Skillet suppers are complete and quick suppers sautéed in and served out of a frying pan. The principle is the same as for One Dramatic Potful—nearly the entire menu in one vessel—but in this case a skillet. Add a fresh salad or relishes and bread and wine or beer, and you have supper.

If marriage is your mission, you might exploit the skillet itself as a symbol of the ease of life played two by two. Point up the fact that the skillet just happens to cook and hold the perfect amount for two—you two. Serve two perfect portions neatly out of it.

As with One Dramatic Potful, dramatize the skillet as you use it for serving. Set it in prominence on your dining table. When possible, sweep off the lid just before serving to show the inviting contents and send out the inviting aromas.

Skillet suppers succeed by their undefiled simplicity— just a few choice ingredients coming together in non-clichéed ways.

CHUTNEY ORANGE CHOPS

Hot corn sticks with whipped chive butter are good with this.

CHUTNEY ORANGE CHOPS

4 small smoked pork chops, about ½ inch thick	½ cup mango chutney with syrup, coarsely chopped
½ cup dry white wine, dry vermouth, or water	¼ cup sugar
2 oranges, peeled and sliced	2 tablespoons lemon juice
	1 teaspoon grated orange peel

Brown chops well on both sides over medium heat in their own fat in a frying pan. Pour off any excess fat. Add ¼ cup of the wine, vermouth, or water, cover, and cook over low heat for about 10 minutes or until chops are tender. Arrange orange slices over chops. Combine chutney, remaining wine, sugar, lemon juice, and orange peel, and pour over chops. Continue cooking chops, uncovered, spooning liquid over them, for about 10 minutes or until liquid becomes slightly syrupy. Serve chops with sauce spooned over.

ALMOND CHICKEN BOURBON

This chicken recipe is easily multipliable to suit more guests than one. And it forms the axis for a little supper (for one guest or more) that is a good emergency supper to have always ready to go, by keeping the few key supplies on hand —in your freezer and canned foods cupboard.

The menu: for a first course and salad, serve canned marinated artichoke hearts on lettuce. With the chicken, have big sprigs of watercress for garnish; flaky butter biscuits (the recipe here is my favorite; but if you're short on time, use frozen ones or flaky butter rolls from your baker); and a tart, bright dry red wine such as Grignolino or a forceful dry rosé. For dessert, have a piece of fairly mellow cheese (something like Wisconsin Münster, Monterey Jack, or Teleme) on top of more warm biscuits, with more wine. Then coffee.

The nonstaple ingredients to store for the emergency occasion: frozen chicken breasts, frozen orange juice concentrate, salted roasted almonds in a can, canned marinated artichoke hearts, a bottle of wine.

This chicken dish is best if you make it with boned chicken breasts. If your meat man won't bone breasts for you (but he probably will, gladly) and you haven't the time, use breasts with the bone in in just the same way. To be best prepared for your emergency supper, purchase fresh breasts, bone, and freeze. (Or use packaged frozen breasts.)

ALMOND CHICKEN BOURBON*

> 1 *whole large chicken*
> *breast (about 1 pound),*
> *split and preferably*
> *boned*
> *Salt and freshly ground*
> *black pepper*
> 3 *tablespoons butter*

> 1 *small can (6 ounces)*
> *frozen orange juice*
> *concentrate, thawed*
> ¼ *cup salted roasted*
> *almonds, chopped*
> 2 *tablespoons bourbon*

Season chicken generously with salt and pepper. In frying pan, brown chicken in butter on both sides over medium heat. Reduce heat to low, add orange juice concentrate, ½ teaspoon salt, and ¼ teaspoon pepper; cover, and cook for 20 minutes more or until chicken is tender and done; stir sauce and spoon over chicken once or twice. Remove chicken to serving plates or platter, sprinkle with almonds, keep warm. Reduce liquid in pan to consistency of heavy cream: cook over high heat, stirring (it will brown slightly). Add bourbon, stir to blend, pour over chicken.

Note • To bone chicken breasts: using a small, thin-bladed knife, make a small incision between the meat and the large breastbone. Using fingers and knife, gently pull and scrape the meat away from the bones; be careful not to tear the meat. Fold loose corners of meat under to form a compact triangle of meat.

BUTTER BISCUITS*

1 cup sifted flour	¼ teaspoon each salt and
2 teaspoons baking powder	cream of tartar
1 teaspoon sugar	¼ cup butter
	⅓ cup milk

Sift flour, baking powder, sugar, salt, and cream of tartar into mixing bowl. Cut in butter to make coarse crumbs. Add milk, and stir with a fork to mix to a soft dough. On a lightly floured board, knead 8 or 10 times. Pat or roll dough to about ½-inch thickness. With a floured knife, cut into 1½-inch diamond-shaped biscuits or use a 2-inch circle biscuit cutter. Place on baking sheet. Bake in a very hot oven (450°) for 10 minutes or until deep golden. Makes 8 to 10 biscuits.

DUTCH WILTED LETTUCE

Here is a skillet salad supper. I like it best for a light supper—with hot biscuits and honey or fruit preserves. For a sturdier supper, have it with dark, moist pumpernickel or rye bread and butter, beer, and fresh oranges and apples.

DUTCH WILTED LETTUCE

1 bunch leaf lettuce	3 tablespoons commercial
About ½ teaspoon salt	sour cream
5 slices bacon, cut into	2 tablespoons vinegar
small pieces	1 teaspoon sugar
2 eggs	About ¼ teaspoon freshly
	ground black pepper

With kitchen scissors, cut lettuce into bite-sized pieces; sprinkle with salt. Cook bacon in frying pan until crisp. Remove from heat. Remove from frying pan any drippings in excess of 4 tablespoons. Beat together eggs, sour cream, vinegar, sugar, and pepper; pour into frying pan, and cook over low heat, stirring, until mixture is smooth and thickened to mayonnaise consistency. Remove from heat; add lettuce, and toss to coat well with dressing. Serve immediately.

MEXICAN PRAWNS AND PINEAPPLE

Serve these prawns over buttered steamed white rice. Garnish with a lot of fresh lime wedges. Squeeze lime juice over prawns and rice as you eat. Drink chilled white table wine.

MEXICAN PRAWNS AND PINEAPPLE

3 tablespoons butter
1 pound uncooked large
   prawns or shrimp, shelled
   and deveined
1 small green bell pepper,
   seeded and cut into ¼-
   inch-thick rings

4 slices fresh pineapple or
   1 can (14 ounces)
   canned pineapple slices,
   drained
Salt and freshly ground
   black pepper
About 2 teaspoons chili
   powder

Melt butter in frying pan over medium heat. Add prawns, green pepper, and pineapple; season generously with salt, pepper, and chili powder. Sauté, turning, just until shrimp turn pink and are tender and green pepper is tender crisp, about 8 to 10 minutes.

PANNED STEAK STRIPS WITH LETTUCE

Border serving plates with orange slices or thick slices of ripe tomatoes. Pass hot biscuits with the former, corn bread with the latter.

Chinese style, have all ingredients sliced and ready to go before you begin cooking.

PANNED STEAK STRIPS WITH LETTUCE

¾ pound flank or bottom round steak, thinly sliced across the grain into strips no thicker than ⅛ inch

2 teaspoons sugar
2 teaspoons cornstarch
2 teaspoons vinegar
½ teaspoon salt
About ¼ teaspoon freshly ground black pepper

3 slices bacon, cut into thin strips
1 head lettuce (butter, romaine, leaf, or head), cut crosswise into ½-inch-thick slices
3 green onions with green tops, thinly sliced
6 very thin slices lemon (with peel), cut into quarters

Toss steak with sugar, cornstarch, vinegar, salt, and pepper. In frying pan, cook bacon until almost crisp; remove from pan. Remove from pan all but 3 tablespoons bacon drippings. Heat bacon drippings in frying pan until very hot. Add steak, and cook over very high heat for just a few minutes, tossing lightly, just until browned; remove from pan. Add lettuce, white part of onions, and lemon to frying pan, and cook, tossing, for just a minute or two, until barely wilted. Return steak and bacon to pan, and just heat through. Sprinkle with remaining onions. Serve immediately.

CUMIN PORK AND CORN

The relish-salad to serve with this: thinly sliced cucumbers chilled and wilted with salt, pepper, sugar, and vinegar to season.

Set table with extra paper napkins and eat corn as finger food.

CUMIN PORK AND CORN

¾ pound lean boneless pork slices (leg or loin), cut about ¼ inch thick
About 1 tablespoon each butter and salad oil
1 small onion, minced
2 ears of corn, husks removed, scrubbed, and cut into thirds

2 medium-sized tomatoes, cut into wedges
About 3 tablespoons chopped fresh parsley
1 large clove garlic, minced or mashed
About ¾ teaspoon each salt and ground cumin
About ½ teaspoon freshly ground black pepper

In frying pan, sauté pork slices over medium heat in butter and salad oil until browned and tender. Slide meat to one side of pan; pour off any oil in excess of 2 tablespoons. Add onion to frying pan, and sauté until limp. Add corn, and turn to coat with oil. Stir in tomatoes, 2 tablespoons of the parsley, garlic, salt, cumin, and pepper. Cover and cook over low heat for 10 minutes; stir once or twice. Sprinkle with remaining parsley.

SHERRIED VEAL STEAKS WITH PEACHES

Fresh peaches are best; well-drained canned peaches are possible.

SHERRIED VEAL STEAKS WITH PEACHES

About 3 tablespoons butter	2 large fresh peaches,
2 or 3 veal steaks (about	peeled and thickly sliced
⅔ pound meat)	⅓ cup dry sherry
Salt and freshly ground	1 cup commercial sour
black pepper	cream
About ¼ teaspoon	
crumbled dried marjoram	

Melt butter in frying pan, add steaks, and sauté over medium heat until golden brown and tender. Remove from pan; season generously with salt, pepper, and marjoram; and keep warm. Add peaches to pan, and lightly brown and heat through; remove from pan, and keep warm. Add sherry to pan; cook until reduced by half. Reduce heat to low. Add sour cream and slowly heat through, stirring. Return veal to pan and spoon sauce over; heat through. Top with peach slices.

CHICKEN LIVERS WITH AVOCADO

The salad-relish: chilled sliced fresh oranges seasoned with basil.

CHICKEN LIVERS WITH AVOCADO

2 tablespoons butter
½ pound chicken livers,
   cut into quarters
⅓ cup finely chopped
   green bell pepper
1 small onion, finely
   chopped
Salt and freshly ground
   black pepper
¾ cup commercial sour
   cream
1 small clove garlic, minced
   or mashed

1 teaspoon Worcestershire
   sauce
2 English muffins or 2
   pieces corn bread,† split,
   buttered, and broil-
   toasted; or 4 hot buttered
   rye toast rounds
1 small ripe avocado, thinly
   sliced
Chili powder or paprika

Melt butter in frying pan, add chicken livers, and sauté over medium heat for about 5 minutes. Add green pepper and onion, and sauté for 5 minutes more. Season generously with salt and pepper. Reduce heat, stir in sour cream, garlic, and Worcestershire, and just heat through. Spoon over hot toast; top with avocado slices; sprinkle lightly with chili powder or generously with paprika.

Sausage Suppers

For a great sweep of flavor, settle into the subject of sausages. Sausages are rarely subtle, but so satisfyingly immediate.

They make their natures so obvious so fast that they are right for the kind of eating that is meaningful, but not of magnitude. And that is how they should be taken—with an easy appreciation, without great concern. That makes them good for suppers anytime, but especially for the late, late ones.

A sausage maker of integrity has already devised the blend of meats and seasonings to make his superior sausage; he has already put into it the major cooking thoughtfulness. As a thoughtful cook, you only have to heat the sausage properly and bring to it some well-chosen accouterments.

And when the pleasures of two people together are as monumental as the pleasures of eating well, sausages can save the infatuated cook. With their small requirements of cooking attention, sausages will let you ignore everything

else but the rapturous indulgence of good food, drink, and the most chosen company.

These sausage suggestions come from European cuisines, where the sausage savvy has built up over ages.

GERMAN VEAL SAUSAGE—BROWNED IN BUTTER

Served with dark pumpernickel, butter, German-style mustard, and crisp red radishes. Beer to drink.

BROWN BUTTERED SAUSAGES

Place about 2 large or ¾ pound German veal sausages (bratwurst or bockwurst) in a pan and almost cover with cold water. Heat to boiling; remove from heat immediately; allow to stand in water for 15 minutes. Drain and dry. Slowly brown sausages in butter in a frying pan.

PORTUGUESE GARLIC SAUSAGE—BLAZED AT THE TABLE

Tucked into a crusty roll. Robust red wine to drink.

In Portugal, in a *fado* house, as a *fadista* sings and guitarists strum, you can roast two big sausages at your table over special earthenware grills—in a sputtering alcohol blaze. When the sausage splits and chars, you slice it thickly, put it into a crusty roll, and pour yourself a lot of the easy-to-drink house red wine.

Here, you can grill sausages over glowing charcoal in a small hibachi or over a fireplace flame.

If you use smoked garlic pork sausages that were cooked in processing, you do not need to simmer them before grilling.

TABLE-FLAMED AND ROASTED SAUSAGES

Simmer 2 large or about ¾ pound Portuguese *linguiça* or other lean smoked pork sausages in water just to cover for about 30 minutes. Slowly grill over charcoal or a low wood flame until sausage splits and chars slightly.

HUNGARIAN SAUSAGE STEW— SPICY SAUSAGES SIMMERED WITH BEER, GREEN PEPPERS, ONIONS, AND PAPRIKA

Served with well-crusted sturdy white bread and/or parsleyed boiled potatoes. Cold beer to drink.

The sausages must be the highly spiced, smoked garlic type, most commonly called Polish (*Kielbasa, Kolbase,* or *Kolbassy*). Beer to drink is absolutely essential to the stew.

HUNGARIAN LESCO

1 *medium-sized onion, thinly sliced from top to bottom*

1 *medium-sized green bell pepper, seeded and cut into 1-inch squares*

1 *tablespoon butter*

About 2 *teaspoons paprika*

2 *medium-sized ripe tomatoes, cored and cut into eighth wedges*

About $\frac{1}{16}$ *teaspoon freshly ground black pepper*

$\frac{1}{2}$ *cup beer*

About $\frac{1}{2}$ *pound Polish sausages, casings removed, and sliced diagonally into 2-inch lengths*

Salt

Finely chopped fresh parsley

In a heavy casserole, sauté onion and green pepper in butter until onion is limp. Stir in paprika. Add tomatoes, black pepper, beer, and sausages. Cover and simmer for 15 minutes; stir occasionally. Taste and correct seasoning with salt and pepper. Sprinkle lightly with parsley. Serve in wide soup plates.

SWISS GARLIC SAUSAGE— STUFFED WITH SWISS CHEESE AND WRAPPED WITH BACON

Roasted in the oven. Sandwiched into a sourdough rye-with-caraway bun. Beer to drink.

SWISS CHEESE SAUSAGES

Strip casings off about 4 small or ¾ pound Swiss or German garlic sausages (knackwurst). Slit each lengthwise (do not cut in two) and fill with a thick finger strip of natural Swiss cheese; spiral wrap with a strip of bacon, and secure with toothpicks. Bake in a moderate oven (350°) for about 30 minutes.

ITALIAN FENNEL SAUSAGE— BARBECUED, SPLIT, AND ON A CRUSTY ITALIAN ROLL

Served with artichoke hearts, mild peppers, and olives (from an Italian delicatessen or canned) and a creamy natural cheese such as Teleme, Monterey Jack, imported Fontina, domestic Münster. Red wine to drink.

If the fennel-seasoned sausages are not available, use the mildly seasoned Italian fresh pork garlic sausages (*salsiccie fresche*).

BARBECUED ITALIAN SAUSAGES

Simmer about 2 large or ¾ pound Italian fresh sausages (seasoned with garlic and fennel or anise) in water just to cover for about 25 minutes. Drain and dry. Place on greased grill over glowing charcoal and brown on all sides.

FRENCH WINE SAUSAGE—
SIMMERED IN WINE

Eaten on a French roll with sweet butter and Dijon-style mustard. Slightly chilled Beaujolais (or other light-hearted red wine) to drink.

For this supper, you need to go to a maker of French sausages (*saucissions*), consult him about his sausages, their contents, their cooking—and get two or more kinds to cook and offer. If you haven't such a source of French sausages, purchase the French fresh pork sausages, seasoned with garlic and wine and available in some multinationality delicatessens; or use mildly spiced fresh link pork sausages and cook as directed below. Or use fresh bulk pork sausage: form into patties, brown slowly and well, and sprinkle with wine just before serving.

WINE-SIMMERED SAUSAGES

Place about 1 pound French fresh pork sausages (seasoned with garlic and wine) in a frying pan with dry white wine or vermouth to almost cover. Cover and simmer for about 20 minutes, turning once. Drain and dry. Brown in butter in frying pan.

Soup and Pie Suppers

Men tend to like pies, and ladies tend to like to bake them. So what more congenial way for a lady to show her care for her courter?

But a little discretion in this display of affection would seem to call for the cook to accessorize her culinary labor of love so it doesn't stand out with its message too starkly stated. Soup is the solution because it makes subtle the passion put into the pie by putting pie into a supper context, and because a fine soup is perfectly worthy in itself.

To stage a supper of soup and pie, let your menu be known beforehand, so your guest can pace himself properly. Present both at the same time, and let the dessert be part of the table décor. Even if the pie is freshly baked or broiled, it can be part of the table setting—sitting there tempting, and cooling just enough while you have your soup.

Actually, depending upon your soup versus pie passions, you can view these suppers either way: soup first—for the sake of a deploringly big pie dessert; or just pie otherwise on the menu—for the sake of a favorite soup.

At any rate, these suppers are of just two items. The cold soups tend to be with hot pies—and reverse.

On soups: the simplest can be the best. But they need a thoughtfulness behind them. The special soups don't just happen.

On small pies: too much crust for the middle is often their problem. The only logical disposition of the usual circular pie for two eaters is to halve it—and that results in an unfavorable crust-to-middle ratio. I have pondered the prob-

lem with mathematicians to try to find a pie shape that
would cut into two portions without an overpowering crust—
without success. A rectangle, halved, still gives more crust
than you want with its filling. So does a square or a triangle
or a trapezoid or a parallelogram. . . . Happily, the answer
lies outside the realm of mathematics and within the realm
of *pâtisserie*: the deep-dish pie and the open-face pie.

PARSLEYED CORN CHICKEN CHOWDER
BERRY CHERRY COBBLER PIE WITH
ICE CREAM

PARSLEYED CORN CHICKEN CHOWDER*

1 can (about 14 ounces)
chicken broth or 1¾
cups chicken broth
1 small can (7 ounces)
whole-kernel corn,
drained

½ cup finely diced or
shredded cooked chicken
meat
2 hard-cooked eggs, diced
Salt and freshly ground
black pepper
½ cup chopped fresh
parsley

Combine broth, corn, and chicken in a saucepan and heat to
boiling. Add eggs. Season with salt and pepper. Heat through.
Just before serving, add parsley.

BERRY CHERRY COBBLER PIE

Serve while slightly warm, with vanilla ice cream—or with a
pouring-on of thick cream.

When fresh raspberries and cherries are not in season,
make pie the same as below *except* reduce sugar to ¼ cup;

substitute 1 package (10 ounces) frozen red raspberries with syrup for fresh; substitute 1 can (1 pound) pitted sour pie cherries, drained, for fresh.

⅓ cup sugar
1½ tablespoons cornstarch
⅛ teaspoon salt
1 cup fresh red raspberries
1 teaspoon fresh lemon juice
2 cups pitted whole pie cherries
Butter crust (recipe below)

Mix together in a saucepan the sugar, cornstarch, and salt. Add raspberries and lemon juice. Bring to a boil, then simmer for about 5 minutes, stirring. (If you wish, strain sauce to remove seeds.) Stir in cherries. Turn into a 4-cup buttered shallow baking dish. On a sheet of floured, waxed paper, pat out butter crust to fit on top of fruits, leaving about a ¼-inch edge. Place on fruits. Bake in a moderate oven (375°) for 20 minutes or until crust is brown. Cool partially. Spoon into bowls. Makes 3 to 4 servings.

Butter crust · Cream together ¼ cup each butter and sugar and ⅛ teaspoon salt. Add ½ cup sifted flour, and stir until smooth.

CARROT CURRY SOUP
Cucumber Sticks or Cucumber Wafers
SUGAR CRUMB RAISIN PIE

CARROT CURRY SOUP*

This is much faster to make than the recipe looks.

1 medium-sized onion, chopped

2 tablespoons butter

4 carrots, peeled and thinly sliced

4 cups chicken stock

1 strip lemon peel (white part only), about 1 by 2 inches

2 teaspoons sugar

About 1 teaspoon curry powder

About ¼ teaspoon salt

About $\frac{1}{16}$ teaspoon freshly ground black pepper

3 tablespoons dry sherry

Toasted chopped almonds

Snipped green onion tops or chives

Sauté onion in butter until limp. Add carrots, chicken stock, lemon peel, sugar, curry, salt, and pepper. Cover and boil gently until carrots are tender, about 20 minutes. Turn into blender container and whirl until smooth. Stir in sherry; correct seasoning. Reheat if necessary. Pour into serving bowls. Sprinkle with almonds and green onions.

SUGAR CRUMB RAISIN PIE

1½ cups seedless dark raisins

¾ cup water

¾ cup brown sugar, firmly packed

1½ tablespoons cornstarch

½ teaspoon ground cinnamon

¼ teaspoon each ground cloves and nutmeg

1½ tablespoons fresh lemon juice

Brown sugar crumbs (recipe below)

Combine raisins and water in a saucepan and heat to boiling. Mix brown sugar, cornstarch, cinnamon, cloves, and nutmeg, and add to raisins. Cook over medium heat, stirring, until liquid is thickened and clear. Stir in lemon juice; allow to cool slightly. Measure 1½ cups of the crumbs and set aside. Turn remaining crumbs into 8-inch pie pan; press into bottom and sides to form a crust. Turn in raisin mixture; sprinkle with remaining crumbs. Bake in a moderate oven (350°) for 35 minutes or until crumbs are crisp and brown. Cool on a rack. Makes 6 servings.

Brown sugar crumbs • Combine 1½ cups sifted flour and ¾ cup brown sugar, firmly packed, in a mixing bowl. Cut in ¾ cup butter to make a crumbly mixture.

CHILLED CAVIAR CONSOMME WITH SOUR CREAM
Crisp Thin Carrot Sticks
HOT ORANGES TART WITH SOUR CREAM

CHILLED CAVIAR CONSOMMÉ

Just barely fold in sour cream—so it stays distinctive.

1 can (10 to 13 ounces) beef consommé or clear consommé madrilène	About ¼ cup commercial sour cream
About 2 teaspoons caviar	Snipped chives

Chill consommé in can until set. Turn into a bowl. Gently breaking with a fork, partially fold in caviar. Add sour cream and fold just to turn in. Turn into chilled serving bowls. Sprinkle with chives.

HOT ORANGES TART WITH SOUR CREAM

For just 2 pie servings, make the filling of 2 oranges, ¼ cup marmalade, and ½ tablespoon sherry.

Shortbread crust†
½ cup orange marmalade
4 oranges, peeled and very
thinly sliced

1 tablespoon dry to
medium sherry or Madeira
Commercial sour cream

Make shortbread crust as directed except press over bottom and only about halfway up sides of 8-inch pie pan. Cut cooled crust into 4 wedges and place each on a dessert plate. Slowly heat marmalade until it melts. Add oranges and sherry or Madeira and just heat through. Turn into serving bowl; pass to spoon over shortbread crust. Pass sour cream to spoon over oranges if desired. Makes 4 servings.

INDIAN SPLIT PEA SOUP WITH
CINNAMON BUTTER
SUGAR-CRESTED PEACH PIE

Cold ale is good with this.

INDIAN SPLIT PEA SOUP WITH CINNAMON BUTTER

¾ cup yellow split peas
About 4 cups water
4 tablespoons butter
½ teaspoon whole
cumin seeds
¼ teaspoon each ground
cinnamon, dry mustard,
and chili powder

1 small bay leaf, crumbled
About ¾ teaspoon salt
1 tablespoon fresh lemon
juice
Butter
Ground cinnamon

Combine in a casserole the peas and 3 cups of the water. Bring to a boil and simmer, uncovered, stirring occasionally, until almost all water is absorbed, about 30 minutes. Add 1 cup more water and simmer until peas are tender and soup is thick, about 20 minutes. In a frying pan, melt the 4 tablespoons butter. Stir in cumin seeds, cinnamon, mustard, chili powder, and bay leaf; cook and stir over medium heat for about 5 minutes; stir into peas along with salt and lemon juice. Remove soup from heat, cover, and keep warm for 20 minutes. Slowly reheat to serving temperature (add a little more water if necessary). Ladle into serving bowls. Top each with a pat of butter and a sprinkling of cinnamon.

SUGAR-CRESTED PEACH PIE

The "crust" for this pie is a top sugar crust. Turn about 3 cups sliced fresh peaches or peaches and plums (or canned fruit, well drained) into 8-inch pie pan. Stir together ⅔ cup each sugar and flaked coconut, 1 teaspoon ground ginger, ½ teaspoon grated lime or lemon peel, and ⅓ cup melted butter. Sprinkle over fruits. Broil about 5 inches from heat until sugar is melted and coconut lightly toasted. Cool partially. Tap crust to break, and spoon out with fruit.

TRINIDADIAN CRAB SOUP
LEMON MERINGUE TART

If you want to plump up the menu, add cherry tomatoes and sesame wafers.

TRINIDADIAN CRAB SOUP

1 small- to medium-sized onion, finely chopped
1 tablespoon butter
1½ cups water
1 package (about 10 ounces) frozen chopped spinach
½ package (10-ounce size) frozen okra, slightly thawed and thinly sliced
½ cup finely diced smoked ham
1 clove garlic, minced or mashed
About ½ teaspoon salt
About ⅛ teaspoon each coarsely ground black pepper, crumbled dried thyme, and crushed dried hot red pepper
4 teaspoons fresh lemon or lime juice
About ¼ pound (about ½ cup) crab meat

In a casserole, sauté onion in butter until limp. Add remaining ingredients except crab. Cover and simmer for 30 minutes, stirring occasionally. Taste and correct seasoning. Set aside 2 crab legs for garnish; flake remainder, add to soup, and heat through. Ladle into soup plates, and garnish each with a crab leg.

Remember this easy shortbread crust for uses beyond this recipe (and the Hot Oranges Tart with Sour Cream recipe also in this chapter). It is a grand base for open, fresh-fruit tarts: Simply fill with sliced fresh fruits sugared to taste, and serve with whipped cream.

LEMON MERINGUE TART

  Lemon filling (*recipe below*)
  Shortbread crust (*recipe below*)
  Meringue (*recipe below*)

Turn lemon filling into cooled shortbread crust. Top with meringue, sealing well at edges. Bake in a hot oven (400°) for 8 to 10 minutes or until lightly browned. Makes 4 generous servings.

Lemon filling • Beat together until smooth and thickened, with rotary or electric beater, 3 egg yolks, 1 can (15 ounces) sweetened condensed milk, 1 teaspoon grated fresh lemon peel, and ½ cup fresh lemon juice.

Shortbread crust • Sift together into mixing bowl ¾ cup unsifted flour and 2 tablespoons powdered sugar. Cut in 6 tablespoons butter until particles are fine. Chill for 30 minutes. Turn into 8-inch pie pan; press into bottom and sides to form a shell. Bake in a hot even (425°) for 8 to 12 minutes, until lightly browned. Cool on a rack.

Meringue • Beat 3 egg whites with ¼ teaspoon cream of tartar and a few grains of salt until foamy. Gradually beat in 6 tablespoons sugar, adding it about a tablespoon at a time. Continue beating until sugar is dissolved and whites are stiff and glossy.

CHILLED AVOCADO SOUP WITH
PISTACHIO CREAM
RUM APRICOT DEEP DISH

Here the intention is a little cold, rich soup and a lot of tangy fruit pie.

CHILLED AVOCADO SOUP WITH PISTACHIO CREAM*

1 ripe avocado, peeled and cut into pieces
½ cup chicken broth
1 teaspoon fresh lime juice
About ⅛ teaspoon salt
½ small clove garlic

¾ cup heavy (whipping) cream
About 3 tablespoons chopped roasted salted pistachio nuts

Combine avocado, broth, lime juice, salt, and garlic in blender container; whirl until smooth. Turn into a bowl, and stir in ½ cup of the cream. Chill thoroughly. Whip remaining cream, and drop a spoonful on top of each serving; sprinkle with pistachios. Makes about 3 supper servings or 4 first-course servings.

RUM APRICOT DEEP DISH

1 can (about 1 pound) apricots, drained and halved, or about 1 cup sliced fresh apricots
2 oranges, peeled and cut into small bite-sized pieces
1 tablespoon light dry rum

½ teaspoon grated lime peel
½ cup each flaked coconut and brown sugar, firmly packed
3 tablespoons melted butter
About ⅛ teaspoon ground nutmeg

Gently mix apricots, oranges, rum, and lime peel; turn into a 3- to 4-cup shallow baking dish or 8-inch pie pan. Mix coconut, brown sugar, butter, and nutmeg, and sprinkle evenly over top. Broil about 5 inches from heat until sugar and coconut begin to brown. Serve while warm. Break top crust and spoon fruits and crust into serving dishes.

Two Cooks

For those who love the art and action of cooking—as well as the results—two cooks cooking can only mean double delectation. It can be about the most comforting kind of sociability.

It can be soul-satisfying entertainment for two gourmets of any age or taste sophistication: for an adult and child, or two good friends, or a flirtatious pair. (For the last, the exhilaration of careful and creative cookery can't help but link to and heighten the exhilaration of a new love.)

The two cooks defined by this chapter do not necessarily have to be active in the cooking; but both eaters must be present at the cooking.

The success of two cooks cooking depends upon choosing dishes worth the making (together) and the waiting (until done).

Some things deserve doing almost solely for the fascinating motions of cooking and the accompanying anticipation of eating. Yet there is no point in choosing recipes that make the time between the idea and the eating agonizingly long. In the following dishes, the cooking is especially much of the pleasure and the eating must be immediate to be best.

STEAK WITH BITTERS BUTTER

This is mainly for romancing—low lights, sympathetic music, good drinks, then something to eat to a man's taste.

The taste theme: bourbon (or scotch), bitters, and beef. The vehicles: old-fashioneds and broiled steaks with a bitters butter.

Or, in another setting, this can be a dinner the guy can cook for his gal. He can certainly make the better old-fashioneds. He can barbecue the steak. And, if necessary, he can charm the lady into salad making.

In either case, have an old-fashioned before and another old-fashioned with your steaks, warm French bread, and salad of orange slices and a few thin green bell pepper rings on lettuce leaves. Coffee later.

STEAK WITH BITTERS BUTTER, PAN-BROILED

Heat heavy frying pan until it is piping hot; sprinkle with salt. Add two 1-inch-thick market steaks (sometimes called Delmonico or Spencer), each about 10 ounces. Quickly sear on one side. Reduce heat to medium, turn meat, and sear on second side and cook to doneness desired (make a little cut to interior to check doneness). Top with bitters butter whip (recipe below).

STEAK WITH BITTERS BUTTER, BARBECUED

Rub surfaces of two 1-inch-thick market steaks with a small amount of bitters butter whip (below). Place on grill over very hot coals, and grill to doneness desired, about 4 minutes each side for rare. Sprinkle with salt. Top with more bitters butter whip.

Bitters butter whip · Beat together with a fork ⅓ cup soft butter, 4 teaspoons each finely chopped fresh parsley and green onions with part of green tops, 1 teaspoon fresh lemon juice, and about ¼ teaspoon each freshly ground black pepper and Angostura bitters.

Make old-fashioneds from a good prepared mix or by this well-tested formula. The main thing is to muddle the lemon twist well to release its lemony oil.

DR. DICK'S OLD-FASHIONED

1 small lump sugar	*2 teaspoons orange juice*
3 generous dashes	*Orange slice*
Angostura bitters	*1 maraschino cherry on*
1 large twist lemon peel	*stem*
1½ to 2 ounces bourbon or	*2 or 3 ice cubes*
scotch	*Splash of soda water*

In an old-fashioned glass, saturate sugar with bitters. Add lemon twist and muddle. Add bourbon or scotch and muddle until sugar dissolves. Add remaining ingredients and stir. Makes 1 drink.

SHELLFISH AÇORDA

Under the aegis of the Portuguese, I learned of their irresistible and original *açordas*—mixtures of bread and garlic and oil, and sausages or meats or shellfish—in unlimited versions. The shellfish *açorda* is my favorite and ideal for two cooks because of the anticipation it arouses as you make it and because its eating has to be absolutely immediate: while the crumbs still sizzle in a casserole or skillet. You top the crumbs with shellfish, fresh herbs, and a raw egg or two per person. Rush it to the table, and stir just to mix; the hot crumbs and oil cook the eggs just enough.

There is an almost intoxicating wafting of warm garlic that fills the air as you bake fresh crumbs to garlicky crispness. Then when you add shellfish, herbs, and eggs, and squeeze on fresh lemon juice, it all comes together with a subtle and savory sweetness.

Cook *açorda* for a supper, and have with it a lot of a full, not quite dry white table wine. Serve it with two citruses bordering—sliced oranges and lemon wedges.

A shopper's note: the fresh coriander is not essential, but it adds the pleasing strangeness. You can usually purchase it in Chinese markets as *yuen sai* or Chinese parsley, in Spanish or Mexican markets as *cilantro*, or in Portuguese markets as *coentro*.

SHELLFISH AÇORDA

4 *large cloves garlic, minced or mashed*	¼ *cup each finely chopped fresh coriander and*
⅔ *cup olive oil*	*parsley (or ½ cup*
3 *cups fine soft whole-wheat bread crumbs*	*parsley)*
½ *pound shellfish (crab meat or crab and cooked and shelled tiny shrimp)*	*Salt and freshly ground black pepper to taste*
	3 *eggs*
	Lemon wedges

In a 9-inch frying pan or shallow casserole, heat garlic in olive oil in a moderate oven (350°) until garlic is golden.

Add bread crumbs, and toss to coat with oil. Return to oven and bake, stirring occasionally, until crumbs are very crisp and golden (about 15 minutes). Sprinkle with shellfish, coriander, parsley, salt, and pepper; break eggs over top. Take to the table and stir just to mix. Serve immediately. Squeeze on lemon juice as you eat.

PASTA WITH PESTO

Anyone who professes to like pasta should be happy to be a part of this preparation. It doesn't take long, and a pasta lover will surely be pleased. This is a grandly amplified *pesto*—with cream cheese, browned butter, green onions.

Pesto (the Genoese basil-garlic sauce) is by far the best if you make it with fresh basil (find it in Italian markets in spring and summer months) and fresh tagliarini (from an Italian pasta maker anytime of the year). In fact, it is almost worth reserving for the fresh-basil season.

Still, if you're fond of *pesto* and pasta, it seems absurd to deprive you and your cooking friend of that pleasure for a whole half a year. This version can shift to dried basil (and packaged dried tagliarini—if fresh is not available to you) without a drastic loss; the green onions and parsley still keep the sauce fresh in its richness.

A dry red wine and this make a feast. Add a green salad and French bread if you wish.

PASTA WITH PESTO

About 2 cups fresh basil leaves (loosely pack to measure) or about 1½ tablespoons crumbled dried basil

About 2 tablespoons olive oil

2 large cloves garlic, minced or mashed

About ⅛ teaspoon salt

About ⅛ teaspoon freshly ground black pepper

2 ounces soft cream cheese

½ cup butter

2 green onions with part of green tops, finely chopped

About 1 cup chopped fresh parsley

½ pound fresh tagliarini (or 6 ounces dried tagliarini), cooked in boiling salted water al dente (just until tender, so it still has some resistance, about 8 minutes for fresh, 9 minutes for dry) and drained

Grated Parmesan cheese

Put basil, oil, garlic, salt, and pepper in blender container, and whirl until smooth (if necessary, add a little olive oil to make a thick, pourable paste). Add cream cheese and whirl to blend. (When using dry basil mix together first 6 ingredients with a fork.) Meantime, heat butter until it bubbles and begins to brown. Stir in onions and parsley. Pour butter mixture over hot tagliarini, then basil mixture, then sprinkle with about ¾ cup Parmesan, mixing as you add. Serve immediately. Pass additional Parmesan.

KRISTINA KRINGLE

This Danish Kringle is absolutely easy, yet it gives the layered and buttery effect of the rich, time-consuming puff-paste Danish pastries. The cream puff paste seems almost a custard in the middle.

The Danes know best about their Kringles: coffee is the best accompaniment. And red currant jelly is pretty to serve with this one; but any addition of jelly should be very slight, or it will overpower the subtle almondness.

This pastry cools fast; and you can even thrust it outdoors to hurry it so you can quickly be about the eating.

In the unlikelihood that there is some pastry left over after the initial eating, freeze it (it thaws rapidly); otherwise, after a day at room temperature, it loses crispness.

KRISTINA KRINGLE*

> Almond cream puff paste (recipe below)
> Butter pastry layer (recipe below)
> Almond icing (recipe below)
> About 2 tablespoons lightly toasted sliced almonds

* To expand recipe, double it.

Spread almond cream puff paste over and to within ½ inch of edge of butter pastry layer. Bake in a moderate oven (375°) for 35 minutes or until golden. Cool on baking sheet on rack. When cool, frost with almond icing. Sprinkle with almonds. Cut into about 12 slender wedges.

Almond cream puff paste • Combine ½ cup water, ¼ cup butter, and ¼ teaspoon salt in a saucepan and bring to a boil. Add ½ cup sifted flour all at once; then beat over low heat until mixture leaves sides of pan and forms a mixture that does not separate, about 1 minute. Remove from heat; continue beating to cool mixture slightly, about 2 minutes. Add 2 eggs, one at a time, beating after each addition until mixture has a satin-like sheen. Beat in ½ teaspoon almond extract.

Butter pastry layer • Cut ¼ cup butter into ½ cup sifted flour until particles are fine. Sprinkle with cold water to moisten, about 1 tablespoon; toss with a fork to mix; gather into a ball. With fingers or heel of hand (lightly floured if necessary), press dough out on large baking sheet to a 7- to 8-inch circle.

Almond icing • Beat together with a fork until smooth 1½ teaspoons soft butter, ⅔ cup sifted powdered sugar, ¼ teaspoon almond extract, and enough cream or milk to make of spreading consistency.

CRYSTALLED NORWEGIAN BUTTER PUFFS

This is a good afternoon baking for an auntie and niece or grandmother and granddaughter, with the prospect of a tea party thereafter. A child can coat the rolled-out cooky rounds with sugar and later fill the baked cookies and sandwich them together. She (or he) can probably make cocoa and whip cream. She can certainly enjoy the feast.

The tea party menu: crystalled butter puff cookies filled with raspberry jelly, and hot chocolate topped with whipped cream.

A sugar coating makes a crystally shine on the surface of these delicate, flaky cookies and a barely-beginning-to-caramelize glaze on the bottom.

CRYSTALLED NORWEGIAN BUTTER PUFFS*

½ cup butter
1 cup sifted flour
¼ cup heavy (whipping) cream

Sugar
Red raspberry jelly

In a mixing bowl, cut butter into flour until particles are fine. Sprinkle with cream, and toss with a fork to mix. Gather into a ball. Chill for 30 minutes to 1 hour. On a lightly floured board or pastry cloth, roll out very thin, ⅛ inch or less. Cut into rounds with a 2-inch circle cutter. Press lightly into sugar in a shallow pan to coat both sides with sugar. Place on baking sheet. Bake in a moderate oven (375°) for 8 to 10 minutes or until golden. Remove to wire rack to cool. Shortly before serving, spread half the rounds thinly with raspberry jelly; top with remaining rounds. Makes about 28 sandwich cookies.

PEANUT BUTTER FUDGE

A father and son or aunt and visiting niece or any pair of older and younger can collaborate on this candy-making—even without experience. It is a simple way for a child to learn the rudiments of candy making and quickly have something to show and eat for the effort.

I first learned this recipe from a mother who makes it for her husband and young son—in an attempt to upgrade their peanut-butter tastes from breakfast doughnuts warmed and thickly spread with peanut butter and jelly.

PEANUT BUTTER FUDGE

1 cup firmly packed light brown sugar	3 tablespoons chunk-style peanut butter
1 cup granulated sugar	2 tablespoons butter
¼ teaspoon cream of tartar	1 teaspoon vanilla
⅔ cup milk	⅛ teaspoon salt

Combine brown sugar, granulated sugar, cream of tartar, and milk in a saucepan. Bring to a boil, then cook, stirring occasionally, until syrup reaches soft ball stage (a drop of syrup in very cold water forms a soft ball that flattens when removed from water) or 235° on candy thermometer. Remove from heat; immediately stir in peanut butter, butter, vanilla, and salt. Beat with a spoon *just* until gloss disappears. Quickly turn into buttered platter or 9- by 5-inch loaf pan, spread smooth. Cut into squares while warm. Let cool. Makes about 18 candy pieces.

ALMOND TOFFEE

This is a confection for people to make who want to indulge themselves; it is absolutely compelling to eat once you've made it or tasted it. It is also a good gift candy. Two gals could make it for their respective suitors—and sample plenty on the side.

Store candy pieces in waxed-paper-lined, covered metal container.

ALMOND TOFFEE*

1 cup butter
1¼ cups sugar
¾ cup whole unblanched
    almonds
4 ounces (4 squares) semi-
    sweet chocolate, melted
    over hot water

¾ cup finely chopped
    walnuts

In a heavy frying pan, melt butter. Add sugar. Cook and stir over highest heat until mixture foams vigorously; cook and stir for 5 minutes more over low heat. Add almonds; stir over high heat until mixture begins to smoke. Reduce heat to low; continue cooking and stirring for 7 minutes. (If mixture turns deep brown, remove from heat, but stir for full 7 minutes.) Pour into a buttered shallow 13- by 9-inch pan (or heatproof platter of comparable area or a combination of pans to make comparable area); spread evenly; allow to cool. With flexible rubber scraper, spread half the

* To expand recipe, double it, and cool in an 18- by 12-inch shallow pan.

chocolate over candy; sprinkle with half the chopped walnuts; cool. Flip candy sheet out of pan. Spread second side with remaining chocolate; sprinkle with walnuts. Cool. Break into pieces. Makes about 30 pieces.

One exception: A Two Cooks project that is not quick to execute.

ORANGE SUGARED ROLLS

The two cooks who bake these rolls ought to be good enough friends to keep company over the three-plus hours of dough rising and baking—before they get to settle themselves around soft and buttery yeast rolls, hot out of the oven.

These golden orange rolls waft a citrus sugar steam as you unspiral and eat them. They call for cups of fresh hot coffee, with the crushed seeds of a pod of cardamom in the bottom of each cup.

ORANGE SUGARED ROLLS*

½ package active dry yeast	1 whole egg
1 tablespoon warm water	1 egg yolk
½ cup milk, scalded	About 2½ cups sifted flour
¼ cup butter	¼ cup soft butter
¼ cup sugar	½ cup sugar
½ teaspoon salt	Grated peel of 1 orange

Soften yeast in warm water; stir to dissolve. Pour hot milk over the ¼ cup butter, the ¼ cup sugar, and salt in a large

* To expand recipe, double it except use 3 whole eggs instead of 2 whole eggs and 2 egg yolks.

mixing bowl. Stir to melt butter; let cool to lukewarm. Beat egg and yolk together, and stir into milk mixture along with dissolved yeast. Add about half the flour, and beat with electric mixer at medium speed until mixture is very smooth, about 3 minutes. Remove beaters; let dough stand for about 5 minutes. Stir in just enough additional flour to make a very soft dough. Place in a buttered bowl, and turn so top of dough is buttered. Cover with a clean towel, and let rise in a warm place (85° F.) until almost doubled in bulk, about 2 hours. Punch down, turn out onto a lightly floured board or pastry cloth, and roll out to a rectangle about 18 by 12 inches. Spread evenly with the soft butter, sprinkle with the ½ cup sugar mixed with the orange peel. Starting with lengthwise edge, roll up as a jelly roll. With a sharp knife, cut into 12 slices, and place, cut sides on end, in a buttered 8- or 9-inch square baking pan. (At this point, you can cover and chill rolls for up to 6 hours. Allow to rise for about 1½ hours before baking.) Cover and let rise in a warm place until almost doubled in bulk, about 1 hour. Bake in a hot oven (400°) for about 20 minutes, until golden brown. Immediately turn out of pan, upside-down, onto serving platter. Quickly spoon any syrup remaining in pan over rolls. Makes 1 dozen.

Midnight Breakfasts

These are for late eating after a long evening out—late feasts in the little hours of the morning.

In 1914, a San Francisco lady and prolific food writer of the era caught the spirit of the thing in a little volume called *Midnight Feasts*, filled with directions for all sorts of salad and chafing-dish delights of the day—for late eating. She puts forth a strong argument for midnight eating:

There are few social relaxations that are pleasanter than midnight suppers, and they have aways had a certain secret fascination, as of forbidden temptations. With those who are fond of fun, laughter and a good deal of nonsense, and especially with those whose digestions are in good working order, there is nothing so popular.

There was a time, in benight ages, when it was considered the height of indiscretion to eat late at night, but in these advanced times, old-fashioned theories are gradually passing, and in eliminating one stupidity after another, we have come to consider suppers at night, after a sociable evening of any kind, both wholesome and beneficial. If we are hungry we are unhappy, and according to the most sensible philosophy, why should we go to bed unhappy, when alleviation lies right at hand, in our pantry?*

More than fifty years later, there is still a mystique and a small sense of wicked indulgence about late-night eating—especially for two.

Late eating is a time you can let yourself go. You're in sort of a timeless world. This is not a prescribed meal, so it doesn't really matter much what you eat. Given just the suggestion, and you can usually set your taste for something savory or sweet.

The only necessity is that these breakfasts be reasonably quick to make—for the suddenly ravenous appetites that can happen in those hours—and so there is time for each other as well as for eating.

SWEDISH OVEN PANCAKE

This is a wonderfully showy oven pancake that puffs up to bubbled brownness around the edge and stays custardy in the center. Serve it immediately after baking, right out of the frying pan, and cut and top it before your guest.

This lingonberry-topping version calls for coffee as the

* May E. Southworth. Copyright 1914 by Paul Elder and Company, San Francisco.

beverage. If you don't want coffee at your late-night eating hours, serve a chilled, almost dry white wine instead, and change the toppings this way: offer a choice of toppings— savory (unsweetened whipped cream and a generous sprinkling of chopped fresh parsley) or sweet (whipped cream topped with a sprinkling of cinnamon, topped with a drizzling of mild honey) or both. You could top the first servings from the pancake with cream and parsley, the second with cream and cinnamon and honey.

SWEDISH OVEN PANCAKE

3 *slices bacon, cut into*	1⅓ *cups milk*
small pieces	*About ⅔ cup heavy cream,*
⅔ *cup sifted flour*	*whipped*
1½ *tablespoons sugar*	*About ⅔ cup lingonberry*
½ *teaspoon salt*	*preserves or cranberries*
2 *eggs*	*in sauce*

Cook bacon in 9-inch frying pan until crisp (do not pour off drippings unless in excess of 3 tablespoons). Sift flour, sugar, and salt together into bowl. Beat eggs lightly with milk, add to dry ingredients, and beat until smooth. Pour batter over bacon in hot frying pan. Bake in a moderate oven (375°) for 30 minutes or until set and golden brown. Serve immediately: cut into wedges, top with whipped cream, then lingonberries.

BUTTER TOASTED MUSHROOMS IN WINE

Serve these succulent hot mushrooms surrounded with thin buttered toast strips. Accompany with a chilled not completely dry white table wine (use the same wine for cooking the mushrooms) and a salad of leaf lettuce cut into julienne strips and dressed with oil and vinegar, salt and pepper.

BUTTER TOASTED MUSHROOMS IN WINE*

> 1 *pound fresh mushrooms, very thinly sliced*
> 6 *to 8 tablespoons butter*
> 1 *cup white table wine*

In a large frying pan, sauté mushrooms in butter over medium-high heat until mushrooms are deep golden and almost toasted, butter browns a little, and all mushroom liquid disappears; stir occasionally. Add wine, and continue cooking until it cooks down completely.

CROUTON OMELET

The buttery crisp croutons seem a little like toast inside the omelet instead of beside it.

Make two omelets quickly, one right after another. Add beer to drink. If you want salad, make a little one of soft leaf lettuce, oil and vinegar, salt and pepper.

CROUTON OMELET

2 *eggs*	*Dash of freshly ground*
2 *teaspoons water*	*black pepper*
⅛ *teaspoon salt*	2 *teaspoons butter*

Make omelet of above ingredients as directed for tomato preserve omelet,† except fill moist omelet with half the

Parmesan croutons (recipe below), fold out of pan, and top with half the cheese and parsley remaining in bag. Serve immediately. Makes 1 serving.

PARMESAN CROUTONS

Trim crusts off toasted white bread slices (preferably sourdough French style), cut toast into ½-inch cubes, and measure 1½ cups. In a frying pan, sauté toast cubes in about 4 tablespoons butter over medium heat until crisp and brown. Combine about 4 tablespoons each grated Parmesan cheese and chopped fresh parsley in a clean paper bag. Add sautéed cubes, and shake to coat.

JOE'S SPECIAL

This is a classic among San Francisco Italian chefs: A ground-beef-spinach-onion-egg-frying-pan sauté. It has to have with it red wine and buttered Italian bread (sourdough is best).

JOE'S SPECIAL

½ *pound ground chuck*	½ *package (10 to 12*
1 *medium-large onion,*	*ounces) frozen chopped*
finely chopped	*spinach, cooked and*
About ¾ teaspoon salt	*drained well*
Freshly ground black	3 *eggs, slightly beaten*
pepper	*Parmesan cheese*

In frying pan, brown chuck over medium heat in its own fat. Add onion and salt and pepper to taste, and sauté until onions are limp. Stir in spinach. Add eggs, and cook, stirring, just until set. Sprinkle with Parmesan.

SWISS AND ALMOND EGGS

Plan on 2 eggs per person for generous servings, and accompaniments of chilled white wine and thin buttered toast strips.

SWISS AND ALMOND EGGS*

4 large slices natural Swiss
   cheese
4 eggs
Salt and freshly ground
   black pepper
6 to 8 tablespoons chopped
   almonds

1 tablespoon butter
6 to 8 tablespoons heavy
   (whipping) cream,
   scalded
Chopped fresh parsley

Place cheese over bottom of 4 individual ramekins or buttered shallow baking dish or frying pan. Gently break an egg onto each slice. Sprinkle with salt, pepper, and almonds; dot with butter. Pour cream around eggs. Bake in a moderate oven (350°) for 10 minutes or until as set as you wish. Sprinkle with parsley.

BACON AND EGG PARSLEY PIE

Serve pie wedges with thick-sliced ripe tomatoes alongside and fresh hot coffee. Or accompany with chilled tomato juice; or, for something alcoholic, Bloody Marys.

BACON AND EGG PARSLEY PIE

8 slices cooked bacon	2 tablespoons chopped
Pie pastry (recipe below)	fresh parsley
4 eggs	1 tablespoon snipped chives
Salt and freshly ground	or very thinly sliced
black pepper	green onion tops

Arrange half the bacon over bottom of pastry-lined pie pan. Carefully break each egg, keeping yolk whole, into a cup; slip, one at a time, on top of bacon. Sprinkle eggs lightly with salt and generously with pepper to taste, parsley, and chives or onion tops. Top with remaining bacon. Cover with top crust; flute edges to seal. Bake in a hot oven (425°) for about 25 minutes or until crust is brown. Makes 3 to 4 servings.

Pie pastry • Sift together into mixing bowl 1½ cups sifted flour and ¾ teaspoon salt. Cut in ½ cup lard until particles are the size of small peas. Sprinkle with just enough cold water to moisten (about 3 tablespoons), toss with a fork to mix, and gather into a ball. On a lightly floured board, roll out half the pastry to line an 8-inch pie pan; fit into pan. Roll out remaining pastry to make a top crust; prick well with a floured fork or cut with a decorative vent.

PUFFED GERMAN PANCAKE

This is one big puffed German pancake baked in the oven. Top it to suit your late-night tastes—with butter-browned sausage slices and chives; or with spiced apples; or with powdered sugar, lemon juice, and melted butter. You present the big pancake in its baking-frying pan, and cut it in two and serve onto warm plates at the table.

Beer suits the sausage-topped pancake, coffee or medium sherry the spiced apples, and tea or coffee the sugar-butter-lemon.

PUFFED GERMAN PANCAKE

3 *eggs*	1 *tablespoon melted butter*
¼ *teaspoon salt*	*Chive and sausage or apple-*
⅛ *teaspoon ground nutmeg*	*spice or sugar-butter-*
3 *tablespoons flour*	*lemon topping (recipes*
6 *tablespoons milk or*	*below)*
cream	

With a whisk or rotary beater, beat eggs, salt, and nutmeg in a mixing bowl until blended. Add flour, 1 tablespoon at a time, and beat after each addition just until mixture is smooth; do not overbeat. Add milk or cream in two additions, beating slightly after each. Lightly beat in melted butter. Pour into a well-buttered 9-inch frying pan. Bake in a very hot oven (450°) for 8 minutes; reduce heat to moderate (375°) and bake for about 8 minutes more or until pancake puffs up sides of pan and is golden and set. Finish with topping of your choice, and serve immediately.

Chive and sausage topping • Cut 1 German bratwurst sausage (about ¼ pound) crosswise into ¼-inch-thick slices, and slowly brown on both sides in 2 tablespoons butter in frying pan. Stir in 2 tablespoons each snipped chives and chopped fresh parsley. Spoon over center of baked pancake.

Apple-spice topping • Melt 2 tablespoons butter in a frying pan or casserole. Add 2 tart cooking apples that have been peeled and cut into thin lengthwise slices. Sprinkle with 2 tablespoons sugar, 1 tablespoon dried currants or 1½ tablespoons raisins, ½ teaspoon ground cinnamon, ¼ teaspoon ground nutmeg, and ⅛ teaspoon ground cloves. Cook over low heat, turning occasionally, until apples are glazed and tender, about 10 minutes. Spoon over center of baked pancake. Pass additional sugar.

Sugar-butter-lemon topping • Sprinkle whole pancake lightly with powdered sugar. At the table, pass additional powdered sugar, fresh lemon wedges, and melted butter for each person to add according to taste.

Sandwich-salad Trays

These ideas are good for lunches or summertime suppers for any two. But they are designed more for two ladies lunching than for anything else.

Unless you are a well-fed and -financed Frenchman, accustomed to long, lingering luncheons, you probably find a salad and a sandwich just about the right items for a satisfying daily lunch. Just those two items plus a beverage can also be the right and sufficient items for a special meal with a special person. But, to let just two main items carry the menu in totality, the food has to be utterly interesting.

These four menus suggest four ways to do it—with just a cooling salad, an open sandwich, and hot or iced coffee or tea.

Tropical Tray of
AVOCADO SLICES, CRAB,
GRAPEFRUIT SECTIONS
CHEESE-TOP MUFFINS

You can mostly arrange individual tray salads ahead of time and chill. Wait until serving time to slice on the avocado and ladle over the nut dressing.

TROPICAL TRAY SALAD

> 6 to 8 ounces fresh crab
>   meat (mostly legs, if
>   possible) or 1 can (about
>   7 ounces) crab meat
> 1 small grapefruit, peeled
>   and cut into sections
>
> 1 small avocado, peeled
>   and sliced
> Crisp lettuce leaves
> Toasted almond-lemon
>   dressing (recipe below)

Arrange crab, grapefruit, and avocado on lettuce on 2 chilled salad trays or plates. Spoon on dressing.

Toasted almond-lemon dressing · Shake or beat together ½ cup salad oil, 2 tablespoons fresh lemon juice, ¾ teaspoon grated lemon peel, ⅜ teaspoon salt, ¼ teaspoon dry mustard, and ⅛ teaspoon freshly ground black pepper. Just before serving, add ¼ cup toasted sliced or slivered almonds; shake or beat again.

Note · To toast almonds, sprinkle on baking sheet, and lightly brown in a hot (400°) oven; shake or stir occasionally.

CHEESE-TOP MUFFINS

Split English muffins, butter, sprinkle with shredded sharp Cheddar cheese or shredded or grated Parmesan; broil until crisp and golden.

CANTALOUPE CUCUMBER SALAD
Crusty French Rolls
split, buttered, and overlaid with
Thin Mild Salami or Ham Slices

Arrange individual salad bowls; bowl containers can be scooped-out cantaloupe shells or lettuce-lined salad bowls. Serve sandwiches alongside salad bowls.

CANTALOUPE CUCUMBER SALAD

1 cantaloupe
¼ cup French dressing
(shake or beat together
3 tablespoons salad oil, 1
tablespoon vinegar, ⅛
teaspoon salt,
1/16 teaspoon freshly
ground black pepper)
1 small cucumber, peeled
and thinly sliced

Salt
¼ cup commercial sour
cream
Dill weed
Crisp lettuce leaves
(optional)
2 hard-cooked eggs, thinly
sliced

Halve cantaloupe, remove seeds, and cut meat into bite-sized pieces. (If you use cantaloupe shells for serving, scoop them out to make a smooth interior; chill.) Pour French dressing over cantaloupe bites, and chill for 1 hour; turn occasionally. Sprinkle cucumber with about ½ teaspoon salt; chill for 1 hour. Drain cantaloupe thoroughly; squeeze liquid from cucumbers. Fold cantaloupe and cucumber into sour cream along with ¼ teaspoon dill weed; pile into cantaloupe shells or lettuce-lined salad bowls. Arrange egg slices, overlapping on top of salads; sprinkle with salt and dill weed.

TURKEY-SLICE SALAD SMORREBROD
CHEESE AND CHERRY (or Cranberry)
SMORREBROD

This double *smørrebrød* menu springs from the Danish design for open sandwiches (which may be as simple as the "buttered bread" to which their *smørrebrød* title relates or as complicated as a many-layered salad towering above a thin sheet of bread).

Here one *smørrebrød* tends toward the savory side with a salad topping of turkey, almond mayonnaise, and romaine; another is more like dessert, with preserved fruit and cheese. The base is the same for both; the caraway twist rolls are frequently available where bagels are sold.

Arrange the two *smørrebrød* side by side on each serving plate. Eat with knife and fork.

TURKEY-SLICE SALAD SMØRREBRØD

For each sandwich, arrange on a split, buttered, and broil-toasted caraway twist (or thin slice of toasted and buttered light rye with caraway) a layer of crisp romaine leaves topped with almond mayonnaise (recipe below), a layer of thin turkey slices, and a spoonful of additional almond mayonnaise. Sprinkle with a few additional toasted chopped almonds.

Almond mayonnaise • Combine ¼ cup chopped toasted almonds with ½ cup mayonnaise.

CHEESE AND CHERRY (OR CRANBERRY) SMØRREBRØD

Spread split, buttered, toasted caraway twists (or thin slices of toasted and buttered light rye with caraway) with overlapping thin slices of a mild natural slicing cheese such as Danish Tybo, Monterey Jack, Wisconsin Münster, or Italian Fontina. Top each with a generous spoonful of red cherry preserves or whole cranberries in sauce.

BACON AND EGG SPINACH SALAD
Tarragon Dressing
CAPER-TOMATO SANDWICHES
Lemon Wedges   Sweet Raisins

Bring this salad to the table in a big bowl; then serve it into two individual bowls, and set each on an individual tray arranged with a sandwich, lemon wedges, and a little stack of raisins.

To increase this menu to more heartiness or to supper dimensions, add chunks of drained canned tuna to the caper-tomato sandwiches.

The lemon-wedge garnish is for squeezing over salad or tuna.

BACON AND EGG SPINACH SALAD

½ pound (*about 1 bunch*)   3 hard-cooked eggs, coarsely
   fresh young spinach   *sieved*
   leaves   6 slices bacon, cooked until
Tarragon dressing (recipe   *very crisp and crumbled*
   below)

Remove stems, wash, and dry spinach leaves; cut into bite-sized pieces if necessary (you should have about 1 quart leaves). Place spinach in a chilled large salad bowl and toss lightly with enough tarragon dressing to coat well. Sprinkle with hard-cooked eggs and bacon crumbles. Toss again before serving.

Tarragon dressing • Shake or beat together ½ cup salad oil, 2 tablespoons wine vinegar, 1 teaspoon sugar, ½ teaspoon each salt and crumbled dried tarragon, and ¼ teaspoon freshly ground black pepper.

CAPER-TOMATO SANDWICHES

Butter thin-sliced white or wheat bread with caper butter made by mixing 2 tablespoons soft butter with ½ teaspoon minced capers. Arrange very thinly sliced tomatoes, slightly overlapping, on each bread slice; sprinkle lightly with salt.

Breakfasts and Brunches

Breakfast is a charged word. It causes all sorts of conjurings up of morning freshness, a new day's appetite that deserves to be served, the roasted coffee aroma and its promise, comfort, daisies on the table, sun streaks, and lovely things to eat: hot biscuits as buttery as shortcake, and honey; mellow eggs, soft in an omelet or scrambled; fresh summer berries and cream and sugar; gentle pancakes with a crispy edge and eggy lightness; the spice of cold citrus; smoky hams and bacon and sausages . . .

And a morning meal for two brings all that about, whether you call it breakfast or brunch (that late-morning breakfast that the dictionaries no longer deny).

Both eating times are invitations to eating anything you like—from just an air-light brioche and sweet butter to trout and bacon or steak and eggs, and to drinking anything from hot coffee or chocolate to gin fizzes and wine.

Breakfast or brunch can be almost anything to eat, but it has to be (1) refreshing and (2) satisfying.

GINGERED APRICOT TART
CAFE AU LAIT

This makes a warming and luxurious little breakfast in bed for an overnight guest. Wedges of a rich apricot tart are succinctly both breakfast fruit and pastry-bread.

So the wait for breakfast won't seem tortuously long, bake the tart the night before. Next morning, if you want it warm, slightly heat it in the oven.

GINGERED APRICOT TART

1 cup unsifted flour	½ teaspoon ground ginger
2 tablespoons powdered sugar	1½ cups dried apricots, cooked just until tender and drained
½ cup butter	
6 tablespoons granulated sugar	1½ tablespoons lemon juice

Sift flour and powdered sugar together into mixing bowl. Cut in butter until mixture is crumbly. Combine ⅔ cup of the crumb mixture with 4 tablespoons of the sugar and ginger; set aside. Chill remaining crumb mixture for 30 minutes; turn into 8-inch pie pan. Press over bottom and sides to form a shell. Bake in a hot oven (425°) for about 8 minutes or until golden brown. Cool on a rack. Gently toss apricots with remaining 2 tablespoons sugar and lemon juice; arrange in cooled shell. Sprinkle sugar-ginger crumbs over apricots. Bake in a hot oven (400°) for 15 minutes or until topping is lightly browned and crisp. (If necessary, slip under broiler to brown topping; cut a ring of foil and place it over outside edge of crust to prevent overbrowning.) Cool on a rack. Makes 4 servings.

CAFÉ AU LAIT

Pour equal parts dark-roast coffee and hot milk into coffee cups. Offer sugar.

Chilled Apple Juice
CHEESE POPOVERS
Butter   Finely Chopped Walnuts
Concord Grape Jelly
Coffee

You sprinkle buttered popovers with finely chopped walnuts before adding grape jelly.

CHEESE POPOVERS*

Beat together with rotary beater 2 eggs and 1 cup milk. Sift 1 cup sifted flour with ½ teaspoon salt into milk mixture. Beat until smooth; do not overbeat. Drop 1½ tablespoons shredded sharp Cheddar cheese into each of 6 well-buttered 5-ounce custard cups. Pour batter over cheese. Bake in a hot oven (425°) for 30 minutes or until puffed and golden brown. Remove from cups and serve immediately. Makes 6 popovers.

Sliced Fresh Strawberries
ORANGE GOLDEN SCONES
WHIPPED GINGER BUTTER
Whipped Cream Cheese
Chilled White Wine
Coffee

For this little wine breakfast, choose a delicate and fruity white wine such as a California Chenin Blanc, Folle Blanche, or Emerald Dry.

Serve scones hot out of the oven, split them, and melt in ginger butter and cream cheese.

ORANGE GOLDEN SCONES*

1 cup sifted flour	¼ teaspoon salt
Sugar	4 tablespoons butter
1¼ teaspoons baking powder	1 egg, beaten
	6 tablespoons buttermilk
¼ teaspoon soda	Grated peel of 1 orange

Sift flour, 1½ tablespoons sugar, the baking powder, soda, and salt into mixing bowl. Cut in butter until particles are fine. Add half the egg and the buttermilk to bowl, along with orange peel; toss to mix thoroughly. Turn onto a floured board, knead lightly, and pat into circle about ⅝ inch thick. With a floured knife, cut into sixths, making triangle-shaped pieces. Brush top with remaining egg; sprinkle with sugar. Place on baking sheet, and bake in a hot oven (425°) for 12 minutes or until golden. Serve hot. Makes 6 scones.

* To expand recipe, double it except use 1 egg. Do not brush scones with egg; just sprinkle with sugar.

WHIPPED GINGER BUTTER

Beat 6 tablespoons butter until fluffy. Fold in about 3 tablespoons finely chopped candied ginger or ¾ teaspoon ground ginger.

If you serve wine at this breakfast, you could break this meal into two courses, with omelets, bacon, muffins, preserves, and cheese the first course; and with additional muffins, cheese, wine, and the fruit as dessert course.

TOMATO PRESERVE OMELETS
Crisp Bacon
WHOLE-WHEAT WALNUT MUFFINS
Tomato Preserves *Butter*
Teleme, Monterey Jack, or Wisconsin Münster
Whole Oranges or Tangerines
Chilled White Wine (optional)
Coffee

If you are hesitant about your omelet technique, make scrambled eggs instead, and top each serving with tomato preserves.

Choose a soft, not totally dry white wine.

Make 2 individual omelets in succession.

TOMATO PRESERVE OMELETS

2 *eggs*	*Dash of freshly ground*
2 *teaspoons water*	*black pepper*
³⁄₁₆ *teaspoon salt*	2 *teaspoons butter*
	Tomato preserves

Beat eggs, water, salt, and pepper together with a fork until blended. Heat butter in a 7- to 9-inch omelet pan or frying pan with curved sides over medium-high heat until it bubbles. Pour in egg mixture, and tilt pan so egg covers bottom. As egg begins to set, lift edges with a thin-bladed spatula and tilt pan so uncooked egg flows to bottom of pan. When top of omelet looks creamy but no longer flows freely, spoon about 2 tablespoons tomato preserves down center. Fold top third of omelet over filling, and slip omelet out of pan onto serving plate, rolling pan so that folded section of omelet falls over its extended edge. Top with a small spoonful of preserves. Makes 1 serving.

WHOLE-WHEAT WALNUT MUFFINS*

½ *cup sifted flour*	¼ *cup chopped walnuts*
2 *teaspoons baking powder*	1 *egg, beaten*
¼ *teaspoon salt*	½ *cup milk*
¼ *cup firmly packed brown*	3 *tablespoons melted butter*
sugar	
½ *cup whole-wheat or*	
graham flour	

Sift flour, baking powder, and salt together into bowl. Mix in brown sugar, whole-wheat or graham flour, and walnuts.

Combine egg, milk, and butter, and add to flour mixture; stir just until all ingredients are moistened. Spoon into 6 buttered 5-ounce custard cups or medium-sized muffin pans. Bake in a hot oven (425°) for 20 minutes or until well browned. Remove from pan and serve while hot. Makes 6 muffins.

Chilled Apricots or Plums
(sliced fresh or poached)
OPULENT HOT CAKES
VANILLA SUGAR   *Butter*
Ground Walnuts   *Sour Cream*
Coffee

These are about the lightest little pancakes in creation. They are superb just with butter and vanilla sugar. But it is even more interesting eating to top them also with sour cream and walnuts, according to your whim. You can make them with yogurt instead of sour cream.

OPULENT HOT CAKES*

2 *eggs, separated*   ¼ *teaspoon salt*
2 *tablespoons sugar*   ⅓ *cup milk*
⅓ *cup flour*   ⅓ *cup commercial sour*
4 *teaspoons cornstarch*   *cream*
1½ *teaspoons baking*
   powder

Beat egg yolks and sugar together thoroughly. Sift together flour, cornstarch, baking powder, and salt; add to egg mixture along with milk and sour cream; beat until smooth. Beat egg whites until stiff but not dry, and fold in. Spoon out into about 3-inch circles onto medium-hot, very lightly buttered griddle or heavy frying pan. When bubbles begin to appear on surface, turn and brown on second side. Makes about 24 pancakes.

VANILLA SUGAR

Store 1 cup granulated sugar with 1 split vanilla bean in a tightly covered container for at least 24 hours.

Sliced Peaches Chilled in Orange Juice
DOUBLE STREUSEL COFFEECAKE
Crisp Bacon or
Thin-sliced Canadian Bacon Frizzled in Butter
Coffee

DOUBLE STREUSEL COFFEECAKE*

Streusel crumbs and liquid make up the base of the cake; more streusel crumbs and nuts make up the topping.

1¼ cups sifted flour
½ cup firmly packed brown
sugar
6 tablespoons granulated
sugar
6 tablespoons melted butter
1 teaspoon ground
cinnamon
½ teaspoon ground
cardamom (optional)
½ teaspoon each baking
powder and soda
¼ teaspoon salt
½ cup buttermilk
1 egg yolk, beaten
¼ cup chopped walnuts

* To expand to about 9 servings, double recipe except use 1 whole egg, and bake in a 9-inch square baking pan for 45 minutes.

Stir together in a large mixing bowl the flour, brown sugar, granulated sugar, butter, ½ teaspoon of the cinnamon and the cardamom to make a crumbly mixture. Measure 6 tablespoons of the mixture and set aside.

Add to ingredients in mixing bowl the baking powder, soda, salt, buttermilk, and egg yolk; stir to mix thoroughly (mixture will not be smooth). Turn into a buttered 9- by 5-inch loaf pan or 7-inch spring-form pan. Mix nuts and remaining ½ teaspoon of cinnamon with reserved crumb mixture; sprinkle over top of batter. Bake in a moderate oven (350°) for 25 minutes or until toothpick inserted in center comes out clean. Serve warm. Makes about 4 servings.

BREAKFAST STEAK AND EGGS PROVENCALE
Buttered Broil-toasted English Muffins
White Table Wine
Coffee

Stack steak and eggs on top of English muffins and/or serve muffins alongside.

BREAKFAST STEAK AND EGGS PROVENÇALE

2 small breakfast steaks (minute or cubed or ground beef patties)	Salt and freshly ground black pepper
Butter	2 eggs
	Sauce provençale (recipe below)

Pan-fry steaks in butter in frying pan to doneness you desire; remove from pan, season with salt and pepper and keep warm. Pour off excess drippings in frying pan, add a small amount of butter, and fry eggs until set. Place an egg on top of each steak, turn provençale sauce over, and serve immediately.

Sauce provençale • Sprinkle 2 medium-sized tomatoes, cut into sixths and seeded, with ¼ teaspoon sugar; set aside. In a frying pan or saucepan, sauté 2 tablespoons finely chopped shallots or green onions in 1 tablespoon butter just to heat through. Add ¼ cup dry white wine and cook, stirring, until mostly reduced. Add tomatoes and gently cook and turn just until heated through. Add ¼ cup butter; 1 clove garlic, minced or mashed; and 2 tablespoons chopped fresh parsley. Gently shake and tilt pan over heat to mix ingredients and just melt butter (butter should be of a thick creamy consistency; do not let it melt down to a thin liquid). Season with salt and pepper.

Slightly Sparkling Dry White Wine or Champagne
HAM-SPIRALED BROOK TROUT,
CHARCOAL GRILLED
BANANA DIAGONALS
Lemon-Parsley Butter
Spiced Peach Garnish (optional)
Whole-Wheat (or French) Bread Toast   *Honey*
Coffee

This is for out of doors, a patio or porch brunch. Charcoal-grill the ham-wrapped trout and banana slices. Pour a slightly sparkling white wine (the kind of crisp wine the French call *pétillant,* the Italians *frizzante,* the Germans *spritzig,* or Portuguese *vinho verde*) or a dry champagne.

In case you prefer not to charcoal-grill, cook the trout and bananas in a frying pan instead: Rinse each trout, dust with flour to coat, and spiral-wrap in *prosciutto.* Fry quickly in equal parts butter and salad oil about ¼ inch deep in frying pan. Sauté banana diagonals just to warm through. Pour hot lemon-parsley butter over trout and bananas as below.

HAM-SPIRALED BROOK TROUT, CHARCOAL GRILLED,
BANANA DIAGONALS

2 *whole trout, each about*	*Salad oil*
½ pound, cleaned	2 *or* 3 *bananas, peeled*
2 *ounces thinly sliced*	*and cut diagonally into*
Italian prosciutto *or ham*	2-*inch lengths*

Spiral-wrap each trout in *prosciutto* or ham. Brush with salad oil. Charcoal-grill over medium-low heat just until fish loses translucency. Brush bananas with salad oil and charcoal-grill just to heat through. Arrange trout and bananas on serving plates, and pour hot lemon-parsley butter over both.

Lemon-parsley butter • Heat ½ cup butter until it bubbles and turns golden brown. Stir in 2 tablespoons fresh lemon juice and ¼ cup chopped fresh parsley.

The Sufficient Sandwich

A fatly and judiciously filled sandwich is the only kind to fit this classification. Such a sandwich is wonderfully sufficient —and efficient.

It doesn't require menu planning around it; it has it all but beverage (beer or wine or coffee or soup). It offers a marvelous way to cut through any pretension—to good eating. And it is a superb way to get favorite flavors together.

The times when two people can take on such sandwich eating is nearly anytime. There is no such thing as propitiousness about it; the time and occasion are up to you and your whims.

Sufficient sandwiches are great for weekend lunches—a quick lunch for the road before a long drive in the country; an energizing lunch in the midst of a bright, accomplishful Saturday; a late lunch on a snoozy Sunday. . . . Or have them after a workday and before an early-evening movie date; as a simple supper when a business lunch was too ample and alcoholic; as the snack ahead of time to see you safely through a night-long cocktail party; as the reviving late supper when there's been no dinner because of after-work swimming or shopping; as that essential sandwich and beer after the game when you replay the game, relive the competition, reman the team. . . .

Compile these sandwiches in ingredient proportions to suit yourself.

WATERCRESS-CREAM CHEESE-SALMON

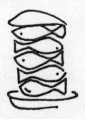

Beer should be the beverage. Little cherry tomatoes are good on the side.

If you use small buffet-sized rounds of rye for this, you can build each sandwich about as high as it is wide.

WATERCRESS-CREAM CHEESE-SALMON

> *Buttered thin slices of rye*   *Smoked salmon slices*
> * with caraway seeds*   *Thin cucumber slices*
> *Cream cheese*   *Watercress sprigs*

DANISH OLIVE-EGG SANDWICH

Make this open-face style, arranging the filling ingredients in deep stacks over top of buttered bread slice. Eat with knife and fork, spreading the sour cream whip over all sandwich ingredients. Beer for beverage.

DANISH OLIVE-EGG SANDWICH

Buttered whole-wheat bread slices

Salt-wilted cucumber slices (peel cucumbers, slice very thinly, sprinkle with salt to season, chill for 30 minutes, squeeze out excess moisture)

Sieved hard-cooked eggs

Pitted ripe olives, halved or chopped

Sour cream whip (make in these proportions: 4 tablespoons commercial sour cream mixed with 1 teaspoon fresh lemon juice, 1 teaspoon thinly sliced green onions, and ⅛ teaspoon salt; sprinkle with additional sliced green onions)

NORTH BEACH SANDWICH

In San Francisco, this is called a North Beach sandwich. Almost any Italian delicatessen there will put it together for you, and sell you the red Chianti to go with it.

Pile up many overlapping slices of cheese, salami, green bell peppers.

NORTH BEACH SANDWICH

> Split Italian or French
>   rolls, sourdough if
>   possible
> Thin slices of young,
>   slightly salty cheese
>   (Monterey Jack,
>   Wisconsin Münster,
>   Teleme, Tybo, Italian
>   Fontina)

> Italian dry salami, thinly
>   sliced
> Seeded fresh green bell
>   peppers, cut into very
>   thin rings

PEANUT BUTTER AND CUCUMBERS ON CORN BREAD

Split squares of homemade corn bread are best, of course (cool corn bread thoroughly for easiest split-slicing); or buy packaged or frozen corn bread, or use light wheat bread.

PEANUT BUTTER AND CUCUMBERS ON CORN BREAD

> Corn bread slices (see
>   quick corn bread†)
> Peanut butter

> Mayonnaise
> Crisp cooked bacon slices
> Thin cucumber slices

SUMMERTIME ORANGE AND TUNA

You can use lettuce instead of leeks, mayonnaise instead of coriander butter. Garnish with ripe olives. To make coriander butter, mix 4 tablespoons soft butter with 1½ teaspoons ground coriander.

SUMMERTIME ORANGE AND TUNA

Thin slices rye bread
Coriander butter
Leeks, thinly sliced
  crosswise

Flaked tuna
Freshly ground black
  pepper
Very thin orange slices

HAMBURGERS SESAME DE LUXE

Have this with a tall glass of chilled tomato juice or vegetable cocktail juice, and you should feel well and healthily
fed.

Broil your hamburger however you wish. My favorite
system is pan-broiling: Heat heavy skillet until it is piping
hot; sprinkle with salt. Add meat (unseasoned), and sear
quickly on one side. Reduce heat to medium, turn meat, and
sear on second side and cook to doneness desired (make a
little cut to interior to check doneness).

HAMBURGERS SESAME DE LUXE

Butter
2 English muffins, split
Sesame seeds
⅔ to 1 pound ground
  chuck, shaped into 2
  patties, and broiled to
  doneness desired
Freshly ground black
  pepper

2 or 3 green onions with
  tops, finely sliced
Thick slices of creamy,
  meltable cheese such as
  Wisconsin Münster,
  Teleme, or Monterey
  Jack
Avocado slices sprinkled
  with lemon juice, salt,
  and pepper (optional)

Butter broken surfaces of muffins generously; sprinkle very generously with sesame seeds. Broil-toast until seeds brown lightly. Top 2 muffin halves each with broiled meat. Season meat with black pepper, sprinkle with green onions, top with cheese and avocado slices. Serve immediately, open-faced, and close with remaining muffin halves to eat.

Significant Snacks

For most of us, it is almost impossible to think of socializing without also thinking of something to eat or drink. But plotting all entertaining events around dinner or some other whole meal gets monotonous and impractical.

This is where the significant snacks come in. They are less than a meal, more than a momentary appetite appeaser. They give an opportunity, if you want it, for eating peculiar things at peculiar times. They entail a kind of eating with élan that two people can enjoy intensely and more might not.

Sometimes the simplest snacks are the best. Here is a cocktail hour that need not go to dining:

Brut Champagne
Roasted Salted Macadamia Nuts

To add a little more substance to this snack, add slicings of a well-aged Emmenthal Swiss cheese.

For a long sherry hour in the late afternoon:

Dry Sherry
CHUTNEY CHEESE PATE
Wheat or Sesame Wafers

CHUTNEY CHEESE PÂTÉ

1 small package (3 ounces)
  cream cheese, softened
½ cup (about 2 ounces)
  shredded sharp Cheddar
  cheese
2 teaspoons dry sherry
About ¼ teaspoon curry
  powder

About ⅛ teaspoon salt
¼ cup finely chopped
  mango chutney (about
  half of an 8-ounce jar)
Finely sliced green onions
  with tops

Beat together thoroughly the cream cheese, Cheddar cheese, sherry, curry, and salt. Spread on a serving platter, shaping a layer about ½ inch thick. Chill until firm. At serving time, spread with chutney and sprinkle with green onions.

When you want the hors d'oeuvres with drinks to have significance.

Cocktails of Your Choice
Toasted Sesame BUTTER PUFFS with
CURRY CHEESE
Almond Butter Puffs with CHIVE CHEESE
Poppy Seeded Butter Puffs with PAPRIKA CHEESE

BUTTER PUFFS

Make 2-inch butter puff rounds of butter, flour, and cream as for crystalled Norwegian butter puffs,† except: press one third of the cut-out rounds into sesame seed to coat, one third into finely chopped almonds, and one third into poppy seed. Bake and cool as directed. Shortly before serving, spread sesame wafers with curry cheese (recipe below), almond wafers with chive cheese (below), and poppy seed wafers with paprika cheese (below).

CURRY CHEESE

Beat 2 ounces soft cream cheese and curry powder to taste (about ½ teaspoon) together with a fork until smooth and blended.

CHIVE CHEESE

Beat 2 ounces soft cream cheese and about 1½ teaspoons snipped chives together with a fork until smooth and blended.

PAPRIKA CHEESE

Beat 2 ounces soft cream cheese and about ½ teaspoon paprika together with a fork until smooth and blended.

A traditional pairing for late at night:

GOUGERE
Red Burgundy

In case you want to do your cooking ahead, you can freeze baked Gougère, thaw, and reheat.

GOUGÈRE

1 cup water

½ cup butter

½ teaspoon salt

Dash of freshly ground
   black pepper

1 cup sifted flour

4 eggs

3 ounces well-aged natural
   Swiss cheese, shredded

Combine water, butter, salt, and pepper in a saucepan and bring to a boil. Add flour all at once; then beat over low heat until mixture leaves sides of pan and forms a mixture that does not separate (about 1 minute). Remove from heat; continue beating to cool mixture slightly, about 2 minutes. Add eggs, one at a time, beating after each addition until mixture has a satin-like sheen. Stir in cheese. Spoon out dough pieces the size of an egg and shape into high mounds on a buttered baking sheet, forming a ring 8 to 9 inches in diameter. Bake in a moderate oven (375°) for 40 minutes or until puffed and golden brown. Serve while warm.

A petit picnic:

CHICKEN LIVER MUSHROOM PATE
Sesame Wafers
Cherry Tomatoes
Dry White Table Wine

Make this the night before you plan to eat it, and pack into a crock for aging and serving.

CHICKEN LIVER MUSHROOM PÂTÉ

2 *tablespoons butter*	⅓ *cup dry white table*
½ *pound chicken livers*	*wine*
¼ *pound fresh mushrooms,*	1 *small clove garlic, minced*
sliced	*or mashed*
¼ *cup thinly sliced green*	¼ *teaspoon dry mustard*
onions with part of green	⅛ *teaspoon crumbled dried*
tops	*rosemary*
½ *teaspoon salt*	⅛ *teaspoon dill weed*
	¼ *cup soft butter*

Melt the 2 tablespoons butter in a frying pan. Add chicken livers, mushrooms, green onions, and salt; sauté for 5 minutes, stirring occasionally. Add wine, garlic, mustard, rosemary, and dill. Cover and simmer for 10 minutes or until livers and mushrooms are tender. Uncover and continue cooking until almost all the liquid has disappeared. Whirl in a blender until almost smooth. Blend in the ¼ cup butter. Taste and add salt if necessary. Turn into a crock; chill for 8 hours or more. Makes about 1½ cups.

Teatime at anytime.

SPANISH FRUIT AND NUT SPICE LAYER CAKE
HOT ORANGE TEA

This cake ages well, and it is better 12 to 24 or more hours after baking than when absolutely fresh. You bake this as a loaf cake, then cut it into strips, and treat each strip as a cake layer.

SPANISH FRUIT AND NUT SPICE LAYER CAKE

¼ cup soft butter
½ cup sugar
1 egg
1 cup sifted flour
¾ teaspoon ground
cinnamon
½ teaspoon each baking
powder and soda
⅜ teaspoon each salt,
ground cloves, nutmeg,
and ginger

¾ cup buttermilk
½ cup cut-up well-drained
cooked prunes or moist-
pack dried prunes
½ cup chopped walnuts
¼ cup golden raisins
Cream cheese frosting
(recipe below)

In a mixing bowl, cream together butter and sugar. Add egg, and beat until light and fluffy. Sift together flour, cinnamon, baking powder, soda, salt, cloves, nutmeg, and ginger; add to creamed mixture alternately with buttermilk, beating well after each addition. Stir in prunes, nuts, and raisins. Turn into a buttered 8-inch square pan. Bake in a moderate oven (350°) for 35 minutes or until toothpick inserted in center comes out clean. Allow to cool in pan for 5 minutes; turn out onto wire rack to cool thoroughly. Cut into three horizontal lengthwise strips. Spread frosting between layers and on top and sides of cake. Makes about 6 servings.

Cream cheese frosting • Beat 1 small package (3 ounces) softened cream cheese with ½ teaspoon grated lemon peel, 2 teaspoons lemon juice, ¾ teaspoon vanilla, and ¼ teaspoon salt until light and fluffy. Beat in enough sifted powdered sugar to make of spreading consistency, about 2 cups.

HOT ORANGE TEA

Place in each cup 1 thin orange slice and thin lemon slice. Sprinkle with about ½ teaspoon sugar; crush together with a spoon. Fill cup with strong hot tea.

This could be a not very rustic miniature picnic on a sunny day. Or substitute tea for the champagne, and use this as an afternoon garden tea.

LITTLE CINNAMON CHEESECAKES
Fresh Peaches
Unsalted Almonds (optional)
Extra Dry Champagne or
Slightly Sparkling, Not Quite Dry White Wine

LITTLE CINNAMON CHEESECAKES

4 ounces (half of a large package) cream cheese, softened
3 tablespoons sugar
1½ teaspoons each grated fresh lemon and orange peel

¼ teaspoon vanilla
1 egg
Butter crust shells (recipe below)
2 teaspoons sugar mixed with ¼ teaspoon ground cinnamon

Beat together cheese, sugar, lemon and orange peels, and vanilla until smooth. Add egg, and beat again until smooth. Spoon into cooled butter crust shells. Sprinkle with sugar-cinnamon mixture. Bake in a moderate oven (350°) for 15 minutes or until set. Cool on a rack. With a thin-bladed knife, gently loosen at edges, and lift out of custard cups.

Butter crust shells • Sift together into mixing bowl ¾ cup sifted flour, 2 tablespoons sugar, and ¼ teaspoon salt. Cut in ¼ cup butter until particles are fine. Beat 1 egg yolk with 1 teaspoon grated fresh lemon peel, add to crumb mixture, and toss with a fork to mix. Gather together, shape into a log, and cut into 6 portions. Press each portion over bottom and about 1¼ inches up sides of a 5-ounce custard cup. Bake in a hot oven (400°) for 12 minutes or until golden brown. Cool on a rack.

Paired Picnics

For some of us food fanatics, the call of food in the out-of-doors almost precedes the call of the out-of-doors itself. Happily, those delights of food and the outdoors come together in a lovely eating event called a picnic.

When there is the prospect of romance, you might help it bloom by a setting of nature and a picnic. Find the country and the fresh scent of green spring and the first warming beams of the new season's sunshine, or the sun-dotted shade of a hot summer's noon, or a cozy cushion of fallen leaves and twigs on a smoky Indian summer afternoon . . . and eat.

When two go on an eating outing, a few but choice things to eat make the best menu.

PICNIC VEAL RIBS, SPINACH-STUFFED
Cherry Tomatoes
Crusty Bread
Fresh Fruits of the Season
Red Table Wine

This veal-breast roast, so favored by the Italian cooks, cools and carves into luscious finger-food rib chops for picnic eating. Each "chop" is a slender rib bone holding veal meat and a savory spinach stuffing. One veal breast serves about 4 picnickers.

PICNIC VEAL RIBS, SPINACH-STUFFED

1 veal breast (about 3 pounds) with pocket for stuffing
Salt and freshly ground black pepper
2 eggs, slightly beaten
About 1 teaspoon salt
1 teaspoon ground sage
About ½ teaspoon coarsely ground black pepper
2 packages (10 ounces each) frozen chopped spinach, cooked just until tender, drained, and squeezed dry

¼ cup finely chopped fresh parsley
¼ cup grated or shredded Parmesan cheese
3 tablespoons minced or grated onion
⅓ pound fresh Italian garlic link sausages, cut from casings and crumbled (or other well-seasoned pork sausage seasoned with garlic)
4 strips bacon

Sprinkle veal surfaces with salt and pepper. Thoroughly mix together remaining ingredients except bacon to make stuffing. Spoon stuffing lightly into veal pocket; close with small skewers. Place in a shallow roasting pan, bone side down. Lay bacon over top. Bake in a slow oven (300°) for 2 hours. Allow to cool. Carve into slices, cutting between bones. Makes about 4 servings.

CONDIMENT CHICKEN SALAD CURRY
Crisp Sesame Wafers
Chilled Rosé Wine
Coffee

This is a chilled salad curry with the condiments right in it. It is sweet and sour and satisfying just by itself. Carry it to your picnic place in a cooler or set into a basket of ice.

CONDIMENT CHICKEN SALAD CURRY*

⅓ cup mayonnaise
1 teaspoon lemon juice
About ½ teaspoon curry powder
¼ cup chopped mango chutney
¼ cup moist raisins
¼ cup salted peanuts
¼ cup flaked or shredded coconut

1 cup coarsely diced cooked chicken meat
1 banana, diagonally sliced
Salt and freshly ground black pepper
Crisp lettuce leaves
1 small avocado, peeled and sliced lengthwise

Mix together mayonnaise, lemon juice, curry, chutney, raisins, peanuts, and coconut. Toss with chicken. Add banana and salt and pepper to taste, and gently toss. At serving time, surround salad with lettuce leaves and top with avocado slices.

PICNIC QUICHE
Orange and Tomato Slices in Basil Dressing†
Chilled Dry White Wine

By the time you get to a picnic site, a freshly baked *quiche* will be cooled; cut into wedges and eat with forks or as finger food. (Or bake *quiche* ahead, cool thoroughly, and chill; it will warm to room temperature by picnic time.)

PICNIC QUICHE

3 ounces well-aged natural Swiss cheese, shredded
5 slices bacon, cooked until crisp, drained, and crumbled

Butter crust (recipe below)
2 eggs
¾ cup heavy (whipping) cream
Ground nutmeg

Arrange cheese and bacon over bottom of cooled crust. Beat eggs and cream together; pour over cheese and bacon. Sprinkle with nutmeg. Bake in a slow oven (325°) for 30 to 35 minutes or until set. Cool on a rack.

Butter crust • Sift together into mixing bowl 1 cup sifted flour and ⅛ teaspoon salt. Cut in 6 tablespoons butter until particles are fine. Beat 1 egg lightly with a fork, add to flour mixture, and toss to mix. Gather into a ball. Roll out on a floured board to a circle to fit an 8-inch pie pan. Fit pastry into pan (if it tears, just press broken edges together), forming a fluted edge. Prick well with a floured fork. Bake in a hot oven (425°) for about 18 minutes or until golden. Cool on a rack.

MUSTARD BARBECUED BEEF
Split Crusty French Rolls
Avocado Orange Salad
Red Table Wine
Cheese of Your Choice

A San Francisco fireman chef taught me this treatment for
a beef barbecue. It is especially suitable for a barbecue-picnic
when the man is the cook. Start with a whole flank steak,
and expect to have a little meat left over. Let the tenderizer
and garlic penetrate while you get to the picnic spot and
heat up the charcoal. Then grill the meat, apply its seasoning, and carve into tender slices and onto crusty rolls, spooning hot-mustard juices over the top.

At the picnic, toss a salad of crisp lettuce (carry to picnic
in cooler or plastic container set on ice), orange slices,
avocados, black olives, snipped green onions, and oil-and-
vinegar dressing.

Three equipment essentials for this picnic: small barbecue
or hibachi with charcoal and barbecuing tools; carving knife
and fork; carving board that will catch meat juices.

MUSTARD BARBECUED BEEF

1 flank steak, about 1¼ pounds (not scored)
Unseasoned meat tenderizer
1 small clove garlic, peeled and slivered (optional)
About 1 tablespoon Worcestershire sauce
About 1½ teaspoons dry mustard

Sprinkle meat generously on both sides with meat tenderizer.
Pierce meat in a few places with a sharp knife, and insert

garlic slivers. Allow to stand at room temperature for about 1½ hours. Place on greased grill over glowing hot coals and broil to doneness you desire (about 5 minutes each side for rare). Remove to carving board. Sprinkle one side of the meat with half the Worcestershire and half the mustard; with a sharp fork, pierce through the meat over entire surface. Turn meat, sprinkle second side with remaining Worcestershire and mustard, and pierce as before. Carve into very thin slices, cutting on the diagonal, across the grain, from top to bottom. Spoon juices over meat slices.

PICNIC RICE SALAD WITH
BLUE CHEESE AND EGGS
Sesame-coated Breadsticks
Fresh Plums (or Other Fruits of the Season)
Chilled White Table Wine

The shrimp, artichokes, and tomatoes are accompaniments meant to be added to the rice salad as you eat.

PICNIC RICE SALAD WITH BLUE CHEESE AND EGGS

½ cup commercial sour
cream

1½ tablespoons fresh lemon
juice

½ teaspoon dry mustard

⅓ cup long-grain white
rice, cooked just until
tender, rinsed, and
drained

2 hard-cooked eggs,
coarsely grated

1 small can (2¼ ounces)
sliced black olives,
drained

3 green onions with part of
green tops, finely sliced

2 tablespoons chopped
fresh parsley

1½ ounces blue cheese,
coarsely crumbled

Crisp lettuce leaves

About ¼ pound shelled,
cooked, and chilled
shrimp (or crab)

1 package (9 ounces)
frozen artichoke hearts,
cooked, drained, and
chilled, or 1 can (9
ounces) artichoke hearts,
drained and chilled

1 fresh tomato, cut into
wedges

1 lemon, cut into wedges

Mix sour cream, lemon juice, and mustard; toss lightly but thoroughly with rice, eggs, olives, onion, parsley, and blue cheese. Cover and chill thoroughly. At serving time, pile salad onto lettuce leaves, and arrange shrimp, artichokes, tomato, and lemon wedges alongside.

*Selection of Thinly Sliced Cured Italian Sausages
and Meats*
Italian Fontina Cheese   Buttered Panettone
Fresh Grapes
Mellow Red Table Wine

A well-stocked Italian delicatessen can set you up for this picnic, except perhaps for the grapes.

Smoked or Corned Tongue Slices on
Buttered Dark Whole-Wheat Bread
Lemon Wedges   Dijon-Style Mustard
SPINACH MOUSSE-SALAD
CUCUMBER SOUR CREAM SAUCE
Raisins
Dry White Wine

A squeeze of lemon juice is imperative, the mustard optional for seasoning the tongue. Unmold the chilled spinach mousse-salads at the picnic spot and spoon on the cucumber dressing. Choose a full and firm dry white wine.

SPINACH MOUSSE-SALADS

1 *package* (10 *or* 12 *ounces*) *frozen chopped spinach, cooked, drained very well, and cooled*
2 *tablespoons commercial sour cream*
2 *tablespoons coarsely chopped celery*
1 *tablespoon grated onion*
1 *teaspoon vinegar*
⅜ *teaspoon salt*
¼ *teaspoon crumbled dried tarragon*

Mix all ingredients and pack into two 5- or 6-ounce plastic or wax-coated paper cups with tops or plastic cups or custard cups. Chill for 2 hours or more. Unmold at serving time.

CUCUMBER SOUR CREAM SAUCE

Combine ⅓ cup commercial sour cream, 3 tablespoons coarsely grated seeded cucumber, and ¼ teaspoon salt. Chill.

Crisply Roasted or Fried Chicken
Little Sandwiches:
LEMON-BUTTER   WATERCRESS-CUCUMBER
Fresh Oranges and Grapes
Salted Roasted Almonds
Chilled White or Rosé Table Wine

Let a delicatessen cook your chicken so you can concentrate on the sandwiches.

LEMON-BUTTER SANDWICHES

Make lemon butter: melt 6 tablespoons butter in top part of double boiler. Stir in grated peel of 1 lemon, ⅓ cup fresh lemon juice, 1 cup sugar, and ⅛ teaspoon salt. Slightly beat 2 whole eggs with 2 egg yolks, and stir into butter mixture. Cook over boiling water, beating constantly with a wire whisk, until thick and smooth, about 15 minutes. Cool. Spread lemon butter between thin buttered slices of firm white bread, crusts removed.

Note • Lemon-butter recipe makes about 1½ cups. You can store unused lemon butter, covered, in refrigerator for 4 weeks or more.

WATERCRESS-CUCUMBER SANDWICHES

Fill thin buttered slices firm white bread with watercress sprigs and thin cucumber slices sprinkled with salt.

Rely on Cheese

The benefits of cheese are many, but one of the best is that it is so satisfying that it needs little else with it. It can stand almost alone and yet give the effect of more than just one item—possibly because most cheeses are complex enough so that their flavors seem seldom to become fatiguing. So you can let just cheese and embellishments suffice for regal desserts or almost meal-sized snacking.

Another benefit of cheese is that wine is about its best companion.

Another is that you can have cheese on hand or get it in a hurry in unexpected-guest emergencies.

The most elegant little feasts of cheese are elegant because they are simple. They are so uncompromisingly simple, in fact, that if you try to complicate them you destroy their splendor.

These serving ideas are mostly from other parts of the world, each one created under the aegis of some sage cheese connoisseur in his own country, with his own cheese that he knows so well.

Preparing these cheese repasts takes practically no effort. You don't have to be fettered by cooking. You can put your energies into handsome serving and setting the select surroundings so that you and your cheese-prone friend can just keep good company and concentrate on the impressions of the cheese coming together with its chosen accompaniments.

But: preparing these cheese events does take some time— the time of putting cheeses out to warm to room temperature—and full flavor—before serving. On a cheese occasion, a cold cheese is a disaster. Serving a cheese cold is at least an equivalent injury to cheese as roasting to overdone dryness is to prime ribs of beef.

The time it takes to let a cheese warm varies with its solidity and size. As a gauge, allow about three hours for a half-pound wedge of natural Cheddar to come from the refrigerator to full taste.

PINEAPPLE AND PROVOLONE

Out of Italy comes the enticing tradition of sweet juicy fresh pineapple with smoky Provolone cheese. There they set a thick fresh pineapple slice on a round of Provolone cheese —and let the flavors mingle. In Portugal, they do a mellower echo of the same smoky-and-sweet fruit flavor combination by combining the Portuguese Serra cheese with fat little Azores pineapples, smoothly sweet.

Serve with a rich ruby port (California or Portuguese).

PINEAPPLE AND PROVOLONE

Place a 1-inch-thick crosswise slice of fresh unpeeled pineapple on top of a correspondingly sized ½-inch-thick slice of

Provolone cheese on a board lined with washed grape leaves. Allow to stand for at least 30 minutes. Carve, with carving set, cutting quarter-circle wedges of cheese and pineapple; lift onto dessert plates. Eat with knife and fork.

HONEY WALNUTS WITH CHEESE

The house sweet at Restaurant Mesón del Corregidor in Madrid (on the Plaza Mayor) is two overlapping slices of the regional cheese, Manchego, strewn with a lot of bittersweet walnut halves and drizzled with a sugary honey. Alongside are served tangy chilled orange slices to flash their citrusness against the confectionery of cheese, nuts, honey.

Pour a medium-sweet sherry if you wish.

HONEY WALNUTS WITH CHEESE

Arrange on plates overlapping slices of Monterey Jack, Italian Fontina, or Wisconsin Münster cheese. Sprinkle generously with halved or coarsely chopped walnuts; drizzle with a mild honey. Eat with fork.

CHEESE AND CHERRY SMORREBROD

The Danes extend their open-face sandwiches, *smørrebrød*, to dessert, and do a stunning cheese-and-fruit flavor interlocking of Danish blue cheese and sweet cherry preserves on rye.

Translated to American eating habits, this is good to serve as an unexpected kind of sandwich for afternoon tea or coffee.

The mood may be a little fancy (make the sandwiches small and serve with tea) or hearty and casual (spread bread thickly and have hot coffee in mugs). Either way, eat with knife and fork.

CHEESE AND CHERRY SMØRREBRØD

Spread thin slices of light rye with caraway with sweet butter, then with Danish blue (or other blue-vein mold ripened cheese). Top each with a generous spoonful of sweet cherry preserves.

RAISINS AND CHEESE AND PORT

The reverence and ritual surrounding port in Portugal require that it is always the man of the house who pours the port. And at dessert time, he often pours it to accompany the rich and mellow Portuguese mountain cheese (Serra) eaten with big, luscious muscat raisins.

RAISINS AND CHEESE AND PORT

Arrange on each dessert plate a slice or two of a slightly salty mild natural cheese such as Monterey Jack, Danish Tybo, or Wisconsin Münster. Fill a small serving bowl with muscat raisins and let your guest help himself. Pour good-sized tulip-bowled glasses less than half full of tawny or ruby port (from Portugal or California).

Note • If raisins are not moist, plump them before serving: allow to stand for 5 minutes in hot water; squeeze dry.

BANANAS AND GORGONZOLA

That powerful completeness and tremendous pungency that are the taste of Gorgonzola seem at once diminished and enhanced in the company of rich sweetly ripe bananas (especially the red-skinned ones).

BANANAS AND GORGONZOLA

Place on each dessert plate a lengthwise slice of banana (or a whole banana with one wide strip of peel rolled back into a curlicue), a lemon wedge or two, and a piece of Gorgonzola. Fork cheese into the fruit to eat. Pass a basket of English butter puff wafers and pour glasses of ruby port if you wish.

CREAMY CHEESE AND FRUIT PASTE

In many parts of the world, the cheese-dessert creators have discovered the wonderful wisdom of putting a creamy young salty cheese with the solid sweet fruitiness of quince or guava paste: in Mexico, it might be quince or guava or perhaps even mango paste—with the local young white cheese, *queso blanco*. In Spain, an old-fashioned finish to dinner is the lovely amber quince paste, *membrillo*, and smooth Manchego cheese. In the West Indies, you find guava paste much appreciated with a salty young white cheese. . . .

Here, use a young, mild, slightly salty and creamy cheese. Young Monterey Jack is ideal—or Teleme or Neufchâtel or even our cream cheese. Purchase quince or guava paste in specialty or Mexican or Spanish food stores.

CREAMY CHEESE AND FRUIT PASTE

Cut guava or quince paste and cheese into slices about ¼ inch thick and arrange, alternating and overlapping, on a serving tray or board, bordered with crisp sesame-seeded crackers. Let your guest serve himself. Provide individual cheese knives and forks.

BRANDIED GINGER CHEESE

This dessert requires that you do something—but not much —in the way of preparation: whip soft cream cheese with brandy and ginger. Then swirl it onto dessert plates and stand in it a few perfect fresh strawberries, pointed tips up. Garnish each dessert with one whole strawberry with stem. Or, when strawberries aren't in season, swirl the ginger cheese into a sphere in a shallow stemmed dessert glass, and top with 2 or 3 dried apricot halves in their syrup (Cover dried apricots with cold water, bring to a boil, then cover and simmer until tender. Add sugar to taste. Cool in liquid.) or brandied apricot halves with syrup. Serve with coffee and brandy.

BRANDIED GINGER CHEESE

With electric mixer, beat 1 small package (3 ounces) softened cream cheese with 1½ tablespoons sugar until light and creamy. Gradually add 1 tablespoon brandy and 1 teaspoon fresh lemon juice; beat well. Fold in 2 tablespoons finely chopped candied ginger or drained preserved ginger.

ANISE-SEEDED GRUYERE

This hails from Switzerland: Swiss Gruyère, fresh pears, toasted anise (or caraway) seeds, clusters of grapes, a soft red table wine (such as a Beaujolais, a California Gamay Beaujolais, or one of the California mountain red types).

ANISE-SEEDED GRUYÈRE

Cut natural Swiss Gruyère cheese and fresh pears into finger lengths and arrange on dessert plates, surrounding tiny dishes of toasted anise (or caraway) seeds. As you eat, dip cheese and pears into the crisp-roasted seeds, adding seed spiciness according to taste.

To toast seeds: sprinkle on baking sheet, place in moderate oven (350°) for about 2 minutes for anise or 4 minutes for caraway seeds; shake occasionally.

(If natural Swiss Gruyère is not available, substitute Danish Gruyère or Italian Fontina or process Gruyère; the cheese flavor should carry a slight sweetness to counter the dry wine and pungent seeds.)

ALMOND-CRUSTED CAMEMBERT
WITH PEACHES

Serve this for dessert, and it is good either with the dry red wine left from the preceding meat or with champagne.

ALMOND-CRUSTED CAMEMBERT WITH PEACHES

Place a round of ripe Camembert on cheese board, and spread top and sides thickly with softened unsalted butter (it takes about 4 tablespoons butter to coat an 8-ounce round of cheese). Coat thickly with very finely chopped toasted almonds, pressing them well into butter. Cut into wedges and serve onto individual dessert plates along with ripe, firm peaches. Pass a basket of hot toasted unsalted crackers. Provide fruit and cheese knives and forks.

Note • To toast almonds, sprinkle on baking sheet and lightly brown in a hot oven (400°); shake or stir occasionally.

Starting Point: Ice Cream

This chapter is for you if you love fine ice cream.

Then you know there's an aura of happiness about ice cream eating that can overlap even to a love affair—and enhance both the ice cream eating and the love affair. Sometimes just one ice cream devotee in a pair of eaters is enough to bring off the aura-of-happiness cloud around you both— as you eat ice cream. If neither of you likes ice cream, it may not work its magic for you, and this chapter may not be for you.

The United States has about the best ice cream in the world. It is easily available. Almost everyone likes it. Most people like it a lot. These verities make ice cream almost invariably successful whether it is dessert, the springboard to dessert dramatics, or the sole excuse for an eating event.

And ice cream is easy to make into just two desserts— without anything left over.

Not all ice creams are suitable, though—not the foamy, frothy ones that are so structured with gelatin and stabilizers that they will hardly melt. (You can avoid them.) The real delight comes in the premium ice creams or some of the ethereal things that the specialty ice cream houses make— rich with real ice cream, smooth with eggs, and flavored honestly with real nuts (not flavors), fresh fruits (not essences), vanilla beans (not extract). . . .

I must confess that my passion for ice cream is constantly refueled by the makings of Swensen's marvelous ice cream store, just two blocks and one corner from my door. There you can get a fantastic double dip cone of, say, one scoop of fresh peach topped with a scoop of toasted almond—on a caramelized-sugar-like cone. You can get a thick lemon milkshake that blooms with soft, natural lemon spiciness. You can get all sorts of other ice cream luxuries and watch Mr. Swensen or an apprentice make his opulent ice cream while you're there. Swensen's is an undisputed San Francisco institution. The Hyde Street cable car clangs by it. The Union Street car traffic rolls in front of it (and often, at the sight and suggestion of Swensen's, slows to the curb for a stop and an ice cream cone). On a warm autumn Sunday afternoon, you might have to queue up in a line half a block long in order to squeeze into Mr. Swensen's and get your cone.

This digression is only to urge that if you don't have a Swensen's counterpart in your life and locale, you set about to seek one out—so that more ice cream pleasures can be yours.

For calorie-conscious or dieting eaters, here are handy rationalizations for ice cream eating: (1) It is healthy. The calories in ice cream are backed up by nutrition. (2) If you love ice cream, you can ignore other temptations, and save up for an ice cream treat reward. (3) Just a little ice cream as topping for a dieter's huge fresh berry or fruit bowl gives the satisfaction of a taste of ice cream (which nothing else will give) and the fruit gives the otherwise needed volume to handle hunger.

Ice cream is a little like whipped cream in its congeniality; you can put it with almost anything, and it will be pretty great. But certain ice cream combinations, obviously, are on the extraordinary level. What follows is essentially a reporting of some ice cream lovers' favorite things.

The following recipes for two are written in large proportions—for enthusiastic ice cream eating when the ice cream eating is an event, not just a dessert.

I suggest that you use hand-packed ice cream, when possible. You get more actual ice cream per measure; and usually it is of superior quality.

PEANUT BUTTER BRICKLE ICE CREAM TART

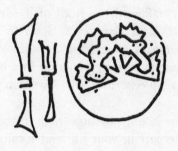

This actually makes three fairly generous servings, but two eager eaters can manage it. Serving a solid half-tart seems somehow gross, so a more acceptable way to present it is to cut each half (or third) tart into slender wedges, fan them out on each dessert plate, and join them with a continuous topping of whipped cream and nuts.

PEANUT BUTTER BRICKLE ICE CREAM TART*

Peanut butter crust (recipe below)
Butter brickle ice cream (or any ice cream flavored with a brown sugar-nut crunch) (about 1 pint hand-packed)

Heavy cream (about ½ cup) whipped and lightly sweetened with sugar and flavored with vanilla
Chopped salted peanuts

* To make 6 generous servings, double recipe, and make in a 9-inch pie pan.

Fill cooled crust with ice cream and spread smooth. Cover and freeze firm. Cut into wedges. Top with whipped cream; sprinkle with peanuts.

Peanut butter crust • Melt ¼ cup peanut butter and 1 tablespoon butter together over very low heat, stirring. Remove from heat and stir in ¾ cup graham cracker crumbs. Press over bottom and about ½ inch up sides of a 7- to 8-inch spring-form pan or over bottom and sides of an 8-inch pie pan. Cool.

BANANA ICE CREAM SHORTCAKE

> About ½ pint banana ice cream, slightly softened
> Butter pastry sheets (recipe below)
> About 1 cup fresh strawberries, sliced and very lightly
>   sugared

Beat ice cream with fork just enough to make a fluffy sauce. Assemble on each of 2 dessert plates: a piece of butter pastry, a spoonful of ice cream, a spoonful of strawberries; repeat.

Butter pastry sheets • Sift ½ cup sifted flour and ⅛ teaspoon salt into bowl. Cut in ¼ cup butter until particles are size of peas. Sprinkle in about 1 tablespoon cold water (just enough to form a dough); toss with a fork to mix; gather into a ball. Roll out on a lightly floured board, shaping an 8- by 6-inch rectangle; place on baking sheet; prick with a fork. Bake in a slow oven (300°) for 1 hour, 15 minutes. While hot, cut into 4 pieces. Cool on a rack on baking sheet.

ROMAN HOLIDAY

A coffeehouse in San Francisco's Ghirardelli Square makes a concoction something like this. It is grand for quickly energizing two ladies, weary after shopping. Or it makes a total dinner dessert—total in size and in being both the sweet and the coffee beverage.

ROMAN HOLIDAY*

4 teaspoons instant coffee powder

1 tablespoon sugar

¼ cup hot milk or water

2 large scoops (about ½ pint hand-packed) firm, rich vanilla ice cream

About ⅓ cup heavy cream, whipped and sweetened with sugar and flavored with vanilla

About 2 teaspoons grated fresh orange peel

About 1 ounce (1 square) semisweet chocolate, shaved with a vegetable peeler in long slanted strokes into curls

Stir coffee and sugar with hot milk or water until dissolved. In each of 2 large sundae glasses, place a scoop of ice cream. Top with coffee mixture, then whipped cream. Sprinkle with orange peel and chocolate curls.

LIME CREAM SHERBET

This makes a good summer's afternoon tea menu for two ladies—or a hot summer's afternoon refreshment for anyone: homemade lime sherbet and gingersnaps and iced tea. The sherbet is creamy and tart with citrus. The ginger cookies are crystal-coated and creviced.

LIME CREAM SHERBET*

1 egg
¼ cup sugar
¼ cup light corn syrup
1 cup half-and-half (half
  milk and half cream)

1 teaspoon grated lime peel
2 tablespoons fresh lime
  juice

Beat egg and sugar together until thick and light-colored. Stir in syrup, half-and-half, lime peel, and juice. Freeze until almost firm. Beat until smooth, return to freezer, and freeze firm (or beat once more before freezing firm). Makes 3 to 4 servings.

SUGARED GINGER COOKIES*

6 tablespoons soft butter
½ cup sugar
1 egg yolk
1 tablespoon molasses
1 cup sifted flour
¾ teaspoon soda

¾ teaspoon each ground
  ginger and cinnamon
⅜ teaspoon each ground
  nutmeg and cloves
Sugar

In a mixing bowl, cream together butter and sugar. Beat in egg yolk thoroughly, then molasses. Sift flour, soda, ginger, cinnamon, nutmeg, and cloves into bowl, and beat or stir in thoroughly. Pinch off dough pieces and roll into about 1-inch balls; dip into sugar to coat. Place well apart on baking sheet; bake in a moderate oven (350°) for 10 to 15 minutes or until they are an even light brown. Remove from baking sheet; cool on rack. Makes about 3 dozen.

* To expand cooky recipe, double it except use 1 whole egg instead of 2 yolks.

THE BEST OF THE A LA MODES

Some established à la modes cannot be excelled—a big warm bowl of Indian pudding with ice cream melting down to cream and into it; chocolate-walnut brownies with vanilla ice cream and chocolate sauce; warm, spiced apple or gooseberry pie and rich vanilla ice cream. . . . But these are all known, and just need to be reconsidered (and re-eaten) once in a while. Following are some of the lesser known à la modes that rate to be ranked with the best.

BROILED SUGAR-CRUSTED FRUITS WITH VANILLA ICE CREAM

This is fast and foolproof. You can use practically any fresh fruit or fruits instead of pineapple and bananas—peaches, plums, pears. . . . The nuts are not necessary.

Serve this dessert at the table: Bring fruits hot from the broiler. Bring scoops of ice cream in a chilled bowl.

BROILED SUGAR-CRUSTED FRUITS WITH VANILLA ICE CREAM*

Thickly sliced bananas and bite-sized chunks of pineapple (or other fresh fruit) to make about 2 cups

¼ cup chopped macadamia nuts (optional)
2 tablespoons butter
½ cup firmly packed brown sugar
Vanilla ice cream

Arrange fruits in a shallow layer on heatproof platter or in frying pan. Sprinkle with nuts, dot with butter, sprinkle with brown sugar. Broil 6 to 8 inches below heat until sugar melts and bubbles. Spoon fruits and sugar crust into serving bowls. Top with ice cream.

In a holiday season, you might like this with eggnog ice cream:

CRANBERRY APPLE CRISP WITH VANILLA ICE CREAM*

1 cup fresh cranberries	½ cup firmly packed brown
2 large tart cooking apples,	sugar
peeled, cored, and sliced	¼ cup melted butter
½ cup granulated sugar	⅜ teaspoon salt
¾ cup rolled oats	Vanilla or eggnog ice cream

Combine cranberries, apples, and granulated sugar in a 9- by 5-inch loaf pan. Mix rolled oats, brown sugar, butter, and salt; sprinkle over fruit. Bake in a moderate oven (350°) for 1 hour. Cool partially. Spoon into large dessert bowls while warm. Top with ice cream.

KAHLUA-WALNUT TORTE WITH COFFEE ICE CREAM

These are individual walnut tortes to embellish with coffee ice cream and two more echoes of coffee—Kahlúa (or other coffee liqueur) on the ice cream and hot coffee to drink.

* To expand recipe to 6 to 8 dessert servings, double it, and bake in an 8-inch square baking pan or 9-inch pie pan.

KAHLÚA-WALNUT TORTE WITH COFFEE ICE CREAM*

1 egg white
⅛ teaspoon each salt and
cream of tartar
⅓ cup sugar
½ teaspoon vanilla
⅓ cup chopped walnuts

⅓ cup graham cracker
crumbs
Coffee ice cream
Kahlúa (or other coffee
liqueur)

Beat egg white with salt and cream of tartar until foamy. Gradually beat in sugar; beat until mixture is glossy. Beat in vanilla. Fold in walnuts and crumbs. Spread evenly over bottoms of 2 well-buttered 3- to 4-inch-diameter baking dishes (or flute about 1-inch-high edges on two 6-inch buttered circles cut of heavy-duty aluminum foil, and fill with nut mixture). Bake in a moderate oven (350°) for 15 minutes or until toothpick inserted in center comes out clean. Cool on a rack. Remove from baking dishes or foil. Put each on a dessert plate and top with ice cream and drizzle with Kahlúa.

* To expand recipe to 6 dessert servings, triple it, and bake in a 9-inch pie pan for about 25 minutes.

OPEN FRESH PEACH KUCHEN WITH TOASTED ALMOND ICE CREAM

It is a sacrifice of perfection, but not too much: when fresh peaches are out of season, use well-drained canned sliced peaches.

If you are short on time for baking, prepare and form the crust part as much as a day ahead of time, cover, and chill. Fill and bake in time to serve.

OPEN FRESH PEACH KUCHEN WITH TOASTED ALMOND ICE CREAM*

¾ cup sifted flour	1½ teaspoons fresh lemon
2 tablespoons sugar	juice
¼ teaspoon salt	¼ cup sugar
¼ cup butter	½ teaspoon ground
1 egg yolk	cinnamon
2 cups peeled and sliced	Toasted almond (or
fresh peaches	vanilla) ice cream

Sift the flour, the 2 tablespoons sugar, and the salt together into mixing bowl. Cut in butter until particles are fine. Beat egg yolk with a fork, add to crumb mixture, and toss until all crumbs are moist; with floured fingertips, press over bottom and about 1 inch up sides of a 7-inch spring-form pan or a 9- by 5-inch loaf pan. Toss peaches gently with lemon juice; arrange over dough. Mix the ¼ cup sugar and cinnamon and sprinkle over fruit. Bake in a hot oven (400°) for 40 minutes or until crust is brown. Partially cool on a rack. Cut into wedges or rectangles and top with ice cream. Makes about 4 servings.

* To expand recipe, double it, except use just 1 egg yolk mixed with 2 tablespoons milk; bake in an 8-inch square baking pan for 45 minutes.

SPICED BLUEBERRY BUCKLE WITH LEMON ICE CREAM

Bake in a loaf pan if you want to serve rectangles, in a spring-form pan if you want wedges.

SPICED BLUEBERRY BUCKLE WITH LEMON ICE CREAM*

2 tablespoons soft butter	1 cup fresh blueberries (or
¼ cup sugar	½ package, 10-ounce size,
1 egg	frozen blueberries, thawed
½ teaspoon vanilla	and drained)
2 tablespoons milk	Crumb topping (recipe
½ cup sifted flour	below)
½ teaspoon baking powder	Lemon (or vanilla) ice
¼ teaspoon salt	cream

In a mixing bowl, cream together butter and sugar. Beat in egg and vanilla, then milk. Sift flour, baking powder, and salt together into bowl; beat until smooth. Turn into buttered 9- by 5-inch loaf pan or 7- to 8-inch spring-form pan, and spread smooth. Sprinkle evenly with blueberries, then with crumb topping. Bake in a moderate oven (375°) for 30 to 35 minutes or until toothpick inserted in center comes out clean. Serve while warm, with ice cream alongside or on top. Makes 3 to 4 servings.

Crumb topping • Combine ¼ cup sugar, 2 tablespoons flour, ¼ teaspoon ground cinnamon, and ⅛ teaspoon ground nutmeg. Cut in 2 tablespoons butter until crumbly.

* To expand the recipe to make 8 servings, double it except use only 1 egg, ⅓ cup milk, and bake for about 40 minutes in an 8- or 9-inch square baking pan.

If you ever indulge in ice cream for breakfast, here is a pleasing plan:

TANGY ORANGE VELVET CAKE

Make this fruit-spicy and velvet-soft cake the night before (and sample a little of it when it is warm, out of the oven). Next morning, cut it into squares; split squares, butter, and broil-toast. Have lemon ice cream alongside, and hot chocolate or coffee.

TANGY ORANGE VELVET CAKE*

½ medium-sized orange	1 egg
½ cup pitted prunes or raisins (preferably golden)	½ cup buttermilk
	1 cup sifted flour
	½ teaspoon soda
¼ cup soft butter	¼ teaspoon each baking
½ cup plus 2 tablespoons sugar	powder and salt

Force orange (with rind) and prunes or raisins through food grinder fitted with a fine blade (or cut orange into very thin slices, then chop slices finely, saving juice; cut prunes finely or chop raisins). In a mixing bowl, cream butter and sugar. Add egg, and beat until mixture is light and fluffy. Beat in buttermilk. Sift flour, soda, baking powder, and salt into bowl, and beat in thoroughly. Stir in orange (with juice) and prunes. Turn into a buttered 9- by 5-inch loaf pan. Bake in a moderate oven (350°) for 40 minutes or until toothpick

* To expand recipe, double it, and bake in a 9-inch square baking pan for 55 minutes.

inserted in center comes out clean. Cool on rack in pan. Makes 4 generous servings.

Note • To add an orange glaze, mix 1 teaspoon orange juice and 1½ tablespoons powdered sugar and brush over cake surface 10 minutes before end of baking.

SOME SUNDAES

Certain ice creams and toppings seem to come together with a dramatic rightness.

MACADAMIA SAUCE SUNDAES

This sauce is also good over sliced fresh fruits—some other time.

You can either serve the sauce immediately after making or cover and chill it, then stir to blend before serving.

MACADAMIA SAUCE SUNDAES

> 1 egg yolk
> ½ cup unsifted powdered
>   sugar
> ⅓ cup heavy cream,
>   whipped stiff

> ⅓ cup salted macadamia
>   nuts, chopped
> Vanilla and/or coffee ice
>   cream

Beat egg yolk with sugar until smooth and thick; fold into whipped cream along with macadamia nuts. Fill 2 sundae glasses with ice cream; ladle sauce over.

BROWN SUGAR LACE

Perhaps the simplest of sundaes: just crumble a brittle and fragile brown-sugar candy lace on almost any ice cream—vanilla, coffee, banana, peach, or chocolate. . . .

BROWN SUGAR LACE*

1 tablespoon soft butter
½ cup brown sugar, firmly packed

Spread butter on baking sheet in an area about 7 inches square. Sprinkle evenly with brown sugar. Broil about 6 inches beneath heat until sugar bubbles; watch carefully. Cool on sheet until candy hardens slightly. Loosen and ease up carefully with flexible spatula. Cool thoroughly. Break into pieces. Makes topping for 2 large sundaes.

GINGERED LEMON PEACH SUNDAE*

2 large scoops lemon ice cream
About 1 cup sliced fresh peaches, lightly sugared
About 2 tablespoons finely chopped preserved or candied ginger

Pile ice cream into 2 large chilled sundae glasses. Combine peaches and ginger and spoon over ice cream.

BAKED APPLE SUNDAES WITH
BRANDY BUTTERSCOTCH SAUCE

Be sure to let your baked apples cool to warm before serving, or you'll quickly have apples and sweet cream rather than an apple sundae.

BAKED APPLE SUNDAES WITH BRANDY BUTTERSCOTCH SAUCE*

2 warm baked apples (recipe below)	2 large scoops firm vanilla ice cream
Brandy butterscotch sauce (recipe below)	Chopped pecans

Place an apple in each of 2 large sundae glasses or dessert bowls. Pour on brandy sauce. Top with ice cream. Sprinkle generously with pecans.

Baked apples · Core 2 medium-large baking apples; pare 1 inch around top. Place in a small baking pan with about ¼ inch water in bottom. Combine 2 tablespoons sugar and ½ teaspoon ground cinnamon, and spoon into core cavities. Bake in a moderate oven (375°) for 45 minutes or until tender; baste occasionally.

Brandy butterscotch sauce • Combine ½ cup dark brown sugar, firmly packed; ¼ cup heavy (whipping) cream; 2 tablespoons butter; and a pinch of salt in a saucepan. Bring to a full boil, stirring. Remove from heat, and stir in 3 tablespoons brandy. Cool to lukewarm.

CHOCOLATE TOFFEE SUNDAE

A chocolate cloaking is a part of toffee candy. For a toffee sundae, the chocolate part is the warm chocolate sauce.

CHOCOLATE TOFFEE SUNDAE*

Vanilla ice cream
Crushed almond toffee (*recipe below*)
Warm bittersweet chocolate sauce (*below*)

Put a large scoop or two of ice cream into each of 2 large chilled sundae glasses. Sprinkle generously with crushed almond toffee. Pour on chocolate sauce.

Crushed almond toffee • Make almond toffee,† except omit chocolate and walnut coating. Coarsely crush cooled candy.

Warm bittersweet chocolate sauce • Over low heat, melt 2 squares (2 ounces) semisweet chocolate in 3 tablespoons water, stirring. Stir in 2 tablespoons sugar. Boil gently for 3 minutes, stirring. Remove from heat; add 1 tablespoon butter; stir to melt.

HONEY ALMOND SUNDAE

To me, this is the most satisfying of all sundaes. For any-one, it is one of the best sundaes—if you like tastes and textures that just overtake you: toasted almonds over very cold, hard, rich vanilla ice cream, and warm honey drizzled over the top. This is for two people with sweet *and* rich teeth; it is almost a cold confection. Peg Bracken in her *I Hate to Cook* mood (*I Hate to Cook Book*, Harcourt, Brace & World, Inc. Publishers) deserves full credit for the idea.

HONEY ALMOND SUNDAE*

 4 *large scoops (about ¾ pint hand-packed) firm rich*
    vanilla ice cream
 About ½ cup toasted slivered or sliced almonds
 About ¾ cup mild honey

In each of 2 large chilled sundae glasses, pile 2 scoops of ice cream. Sprinkle with almonds. Heat honey just until it begins to bubble; pour over ice cream.

Note • To toast almonds, sprinkle on baking sheet and lightly brown in a hot (400°) oven; shake or stir occasionally.

COPENHAGEN SUNDAE

Five years after the event, I found a travel-eating-note to myself labeled, "Denmark Treat." The treat had happened in the Berry Cellar, a little sweets and ice cream shop down some steps and into a tiny doorway off one of Copenhagen's shoppers' streets. The treat was rich vanilla ice cream with spicy red raspberries on top of it, and hot chocolate alongside. Here, for two, crisp cinnamon-nut cookies complete a sweet feast.

COPENHAGEN SUNDAE*

Fresh red raspberries   Sugar   Rich vanilla ice cream

Gently toss raspberries with sugar to sweeten. Chill for 1 hour or more. Fill 2 sundae glasses with vanilla ice cream. Top with raspberries.

These are the best ice cream cookies whether your ice cream is a sundae or not.

CINNAMON NUT CRISPS*

½ cup soft butter
½ cup sugar
1 egg yolk
1 cup sifted flour

½ teaspoon ground
cinnamon
½ cup finely chopped
pecans, almonds, or
walnuts

Cream butter and sugar. Beat in half the egg yolk thoroughly. Sift flour with cinnamon into creamed mixture, and stir or beat in thoroughly. Spread in an even layer over bottom of 8-inch square baking pan. Beat remaining egg yolk slightly; brush over top. With fingertips, smooth surface. Sprinkle nuts over dough, and press in. Bake in a very slow oven (275°) for 1 hour. While hot, cut into about 25 squares. Cool on a rack.

* To expand recipe, double it except use only 1 egg, with yolk in dough and slightly beaten egg white over top of the dough; bake in a 15- by 10-inch pan.

The Party Crêpe

Master the crêpe and anything dramatic can follow. The crêpe, just by its delicate, elegant nature, seems to have built-in style.

Once you have this culinary specialty within your command, it can become the building block for all sorts of regal desserts and exotic presentations of seafood, meat, vegetables, cheeses. . . . In fact, the crêpe is so spectacular that it can be the axis point for designing parties.

This chapter outlines three specific crêpe parties (written here as parties for two, but easily expandable for many more)—a dessert party, a brunch, a cocktail supper. (You can certainly use the crêpe recipes at plenty of other times besides parties; some suggestions follow.)

Acquiring the crêpe culinary specialty doesn't call for tricks or talents. It just calls for a fine recipe, a pan, ingredients, and some good ideas about the disposition of the finished, eggy, thin pancakes. Besides the ease of making, crêpes have added boons: you can make them ahead of time (often fill) and just heat before serving. Crêpes freeze well; you can make them ahead to have always on hand—and they even thaw quickly.

It is my zeal for crêpes that prompted the listing of a crêpe pan with basic cooking equipment (Starting Out chapter). Usually, in cooking for two, I would not recommend buying special equipment for special dishes; the crêpe pan is the exception. Another frying pan with shallow, rounded edges can be made to work, but it is more difficult. A crêpe pan is so specifically designed for turning out proper crêpes that it is worth the small investment: the shallow, flared sides make it easy to get hold of the crêpe to turn it; the long handle helps you tilt the batter all over the pan bottom; the cast-iron material takes well to seasoning to a glowing, butter-burnished surface so crêpes will not stick.

A QUICK LESSON ON THE BASIC CREPE

Before you begin, season a new cast-iron crêpe pan: wash and dry pan. Rub well with shortening or salad oil, and place in a slow oven (200°) for 1½ hours. Allow to cool in oven. Wash with water and dry immediately. After each use, wash pan with mild soap and water (never scour), and dry immediately.

If you wish, mix the crêpe batter 30 minutes before using; during that time, batter becomes *slightly* smoother and *slightly* easier to work with.

Use a long, thin flexible spatula for easiest turning.

Don't be afraid of crêpes; they are truly simple. Follow this recipe:

CRÊPES

2 eggs
4 tablespoons flour
¼ teaspoon salt

⅔ cup milk
Butter (about 2
    tablespoons)

Beat eggs slightly. Add flour and salt and beat until smooth. Gradually add milk, beating until batter is smooth. (Cover and chill for 30 minutes if you wish; stir to blend well before using.) Heat butter (½ to 1 teaspoon for each pancake) over medium-high heat in 7- to 8-inch crêpe pan. Pour in about 3 tablespoons batter; quickly tilt and rotate pan so batter covers bottom. When lightly brown on bottom, turn and lightly brown on second side. Slip onto plate or clean towel. Makes about 8 crêpes.

If you make crêpes a day or several hours ahead of serving: thoroughly cool baked crêpes, stack (a piece of foil or waxed paper between makes separating easy), cover or wrap, and chill.

If you make crêpes more than a day in advance, freeze them: stack cooled crêpes with a sheet of foil separating them. Wrap airtight in a plastic freezer bag or heavy foil. Freeze. Allow to thaw completely before using. (A stack of 6 frozen crêpes takes about 1 hour to thaw at room temperature.)

For all the party crêpe recipes below, you can fill the baked crêpes several hours before the party and cover and refrigerate. If you do this, take crêpes out of refrigerator long enough before party time to return to room temperature; or plan to bake longer than directed.

A CREPE DESSERT PARTY

Chill champagne in the refrigerator for two to four hours before serving. Allow one-fifth for two. Serve it before and during the crêpe eating.

If possible, heat both kinds of crêpes together on heating-serving platter.

To simplify the menu, you could use just one kind of crêpe; if you choose the walnut one, you could offer only the whipped cream, and sprinkle it with grated chocolate.

To expand this menu for more guests, just multiply recipe proportions.

For occasions outside this particular party, you can use each dessert-crêpe recipe for a dinner or luncheon dessert; two filled crêpes are enough for a dinner dessert serving.

Chilled Extra Dry Champagne
ORANGE WALNUT CREPES *with*
RUM WHIPPED CREAM *and*
RUM CHOCOLATE SAUCE
CREAM CHEESE CREPES *with*
Toasted Almonds and APRICOT SAUCE
Coffee

ORANGE WALNUT CRÊPES

½ cup sugar	*About 1 teaspoon grated*
⅓ cup ground walnuts	*fresh orange peel*
1 tablespoon light rum	*4 crêpes*
1 tablespoon moist raisins	*About 1½ teaspoons butter*
(preferably golden)	

Mix sugar, walnuts, rum, raisins, and ¼ teaspoon of the orange peel. Spread almost to edge of each crêpe. Fold in 2 ends, and roll up each crêpe. Place on buttered baking-serving platter (or in shallow baking pan). Dot with butter. Bake in a moderate oven (350°) for 10 minutes or until heated through. Sprinkle with remaining orange peel.

RUM WHIPPED CREAM

Whip cream and sweeten with sugar and flavor with light rum.

RUM CHOCOLATE SAUCE

Partially melt 2 squares (2 ounces) semisweet chocolate over hot water in top part of double boiler. Stir until smooth. Gradually stir in 4 tablespoons commercial sour cream and 2 tablespoons light rum. Heat through.

CREAM CHEESE CRÊPES

1 *small package (3 ounces)*	*4 crêpes*
cream cheese, softened	*About 1½ teaspoons butter*
2 *tablespoons soft butter*	*About 2 tablespoons*
2 *tablespoons sugar*	*toasted slivered or sliced*
½ *teaspoon vanilla*	*almonds*

Beat cheese, the 2 tablespoons butter, sugar, and vanilla together until light and fluffy. Spread almost to edge of each crêpe. Fold in 2 ends and roll up each crêpe. Arrange on buttered baking-serving platter. Dot with remaining butter. Bake in a moderate oven (350°) for 10 minutes or until heated through. Sprinkle with almonds.

APRICOT SAUCE

Combine in a saucepan ¼ cup apricot jam, 2 tablespoons orange juice, 1 tablespoon butter, ½ teaspoon grated lemon peel, and 1 teaspoon lemon juice. Heat together, stirring.

A CREPE COCKTAIL SUPPER

Cocktails   Toasted Salted Almonds and/or Filberts
LAYERED HAM CREPES
ORANGE AND TOMATO SLICES IN
BASIL DRESSING
Chilled Dry Rosé
COFFEE ICE CREAM TOPPED WITH
BROWN-SUGARED APRICOTS
Coffee

LAYERED HAM CRÊPES*

Here you cut a stack of crêpes, layered with a ham-sour cream filling, into wedges to serve.

*½ pound cooked smoked
 ham, ground or finely
 minced*
*About ¾ cup commercial
 sour cream*
*3 green onions with part
 of green tops, finely
 chopped*

*¼ teaspoon Dijon-style
 mustard*
About ⅛ teaspoon salt
*About ⅛ teaspoon freshly
 ground black pepper*
6 crêpes
About 1 tablespoon butter

* To expand the recipe to 4 large servings or 6 small servings, double it
except build it into a 12-crêpe stack and bake for 20 minutes.

Combine ham, ½ cup sour cream, half the onions, the mustard, salt, and pepper. Place 1 crêpe on buttered baking-serving platter. Spread almost to edges with a thin layer of ham mixture. Repeat, using all ham mixture and crêpes. Dot top crêpe with butter. Bake in a moderate oven (350°) for 15 minutes. Garnish top with spoonfuls of remaining sour cream; sprinkle with remaining green onions.

ORANGE AND TOMATO SLICES IN BASIL DRESSING

Cut 1 large tomato and 1 large peeled orange into thin cross-wise slices. Shake or beat together ¼ cup salad oil, 1 table-spoon wine vinegar, ⅛ teaspoon salt, ⅛ teaspoon crumbled dried basil, and ¹⁄₁₆ teaspoon each sugar and freshly ground black pepper; pour over tomato and orange. Cover and chill for 1 hour or more. At serving time, arrange orange and tomato slices on lettuce; spoon dressing over.

COFFEE ICE CREAM TOPPED WITH BROWN-SUGARED APRICOTS

Place dried apricots (about ¼ cup) in saucepan with cold water to cover. Bring to a boil, then cover and simmer until tender. Add brown sugar to sweeten; allow to cool; then chill. Spoon apricots and sauce over scoops of coffee ice cream, sundae style.

A CREPE AND SAUSAGE BRUNCH

The following twosome recipe proportions are for a couple with good morning appetites and/or a long time for eating. For a party bigger than two, you can plan on only two spinach crêpes per person.

Spinach crêpes outside the party realm: serve as a dinner first course or as the dinner vegetable alongside a broiled pork or lamb chop.

GOOD OLD MAC'S GIN FIZZES
BUTTER-BROWNED SAUSAGES
Roll-ups of Thin-sliced Italian Coppa (optional)
(or Other Cured Sausages)
SPINACH PARMESAN CREPES
Buttered Toasted English Muffins (optional)
Fresh Tomato Wedges
WARM DATE COFFEECAKE with
SLICED FRESH PEACHES and *Whipped Cream*
Coffee

A perfect gin fizz is a rare thing. These gin fizzes bear the name of the persevering scholar who willingly accepted all risks of time and tasting to create the fine fizz that has become the standard for himself and his friends.

GOOD OLD MAC'S GIN FIZZES

4 ounces (½ cup) gin

3 ounces (6 tablespoons) half-and-half (half milk and half cream)

1½ ounces (3 tablespoons) fresh lemon juice

1 ounce (2 tablespoons) orange juice

1 tablespoon sugar

1 egg

3 drops orange flower water

1 handful (about ⅓ cup) crushed ice

Combine all ingredients in blender container and whirl until smooth. Serve immediately in chilled glasses. Makes 2 large drinks.

BUTTER-BROWNED SAUSAGES

Purchase about ¼ pound Italian fennel sausages, French wine sausages, or other mildly spicy fresh link sausage per person. Place in a frying pan with equal parts dry white wine and water almost to cover. Heat just to boiling point, then cover and simmer until done (about 20 minutes for inch-thick sausages). Pour off liquid. Add a small amount of butter to frying pan, and slowly brown sausages on all sides.

SPINACH PARMESAN CRÊPES

4 green onions with part of green tops, finely chopped
2 tablespoons butter
1 package (10 ounces) chopped frozen spinach, cooked until tender, drained, and squeezed dry
1 teaspoon lemon juice
⅜ teaspoon salt
¼ teaspoon ground sage
⅛ teaspoon ground nutmeg
About ¹⁄₁₆ teaspoon freshly ground black pepper
6 crêpes
¼ cup grated or shredded Parmesan cheese
About 1 tablespoon butter

In a frying pan, sauté onions in butter until limp. Remove from heat and stir in spinach, lemon juice, salt, sage, nutmeg, and pepper. Spread almost to edge of each crêpe. Fold in 2 ends of each crêpe, and roll up. Place on a buttered baking-serving platter. Sprinkle with Parmesan. Dot with butter. Bake in a moderate oven (350°) for 10 minutes or until heated through.

WARM DATE COFFEECAKE*

This is really fast to make.

½ cup pitted dates, cut up   ½ teaspoon vanilla
½ teaspoon soda   ¾ cup sifted flour
½ cup boiling water   ½ teaspoon baking powder
¼ cup butter   Coconut-sugar topping
1 egg   (recipe below)
½ cup sugar

In a large mixing bowl, toss dates with soda. Add water and butter and stir until butter is melted; set aside to cool to lukewarm. Beat egg, then beat in sugar and vanilla; stir into cooled date mixture. Sift flour with baking powder into date mixture; stir to mix well. Turn into buttered 9- by 5-inch loaf pan. Bake in a moderate oven (350°) for 20 minutes. Sprinkle coconut-sugar topping evenly over top; bake 10 to 15 minutes more, until topping is golden brown. Partially cool on a rack. Cut into squares or rectangles. Makes 4 servings.

Coconut-sugar topping · Combine ½ cup flaked or shredded coconut; ½ cup brown sugar, firmly packed; 1 tablespoon heavy cream; and 1 tablespoon melted butter.

SLICED FRESH PEACHES

Sprinkle with sugar to taste. Serve in a bowl, and let guest spoon them alongside coffeecake. When fresh peaches are out of season, substitute sliced canned or frozen (thawed) peaches, well drained.

* To expand recipe, double it except use only 1 egg, bake in a 9-inch square pan for 25 minutes before adding topping, and cut into 8 to 10 servings.

Index

4